"How do you get and keep your customers' attention in order to create one-to-one relationships? **Put *Simplicity* into the hands of every employee.** It will help them work smarter and learn to focus on what's really important— your customers."

> **DON PEPPERS,** co-founder of Peppers and Rogers Group and co-author of *The One to One Future, Enterprise One to One* and *The One to One Manager*

"*Simplicity* offers the response to the question: **What happens when more-better-faster meets enough-is-enough?** Business leaders trying to attract and retain the best people in their field will get practical lessons and tools for creating work environments where what you do is just as important as how you do it."

> **PETER D. MOORE,** Managing Partner, Inferential Focus; author of *The Caterpillar Doesn't Know: How Personal Change Is Driving Organizational Change*

"**A breakthrough in the design of understanding. A must read!** In a world of infinite choices, *Simplicity* provides clarity and focus. Most important, Bill Jensen empowers us to act with confidence without feeling guilty."

> **CLEMENT MOK,** Chief Creative Officer, Sapient

"**Bill Jensen combines thinking about work processes, knowledge management, and even business strategy** to create a unique perspective on business. *Simplicity* is an enlightening and entertaining book on the complex topic of creating simpler work. "

> **THOMAS H. DAVENPORT,** Director, Andersen Consulting Institute for Strategic Change; Professor, Boston University School of Management

"Bill Jensen looks at the human side—what the workforce needs. Things are too complex. He lays out an organized plan to cut through the mess, or to completely eliminate it. **He understands what we Net Geners need**—what worked for corporate leaders in the past won't work for us now."

> **JENNY MAE KHO,** senior, Sharon High School, Massachusetts

"*Simplicity* makes the case. **For those companies that can follow what Bill Jensen has laid out—putting learning and work back together— the future is theirs.** Practice the future."

> **SUSAN U. STUCKY,** Director, Strategic Practices Group at the Institute for Research on Learning

"The elegance of simplicity is Bill Jensen's book. It spoke to the weight of complexity of my many assignments. To paraphrase William Blake—after reading *Simplicity,* I put infinity into the palm of my hand."

> **STANLEY S. GRYSKIEWICZ,** Senior Fellow, Innovation and Creativity Center for Creative Leadership and author of *Positive Turbulence: Developing Climates for Creativity, Innovation, and Renewal*

"Bill Jensen is the Studs Terkel of knowledge workers. To read *Simplicity* is to understand workaday clarity, common sense, and smart choices in a complex world. **Rediscover your sense of purpose and energy.** Read this book and ask new questions."

> **HUBERT SAINT-ONGE,** Senior Vice President, Strategic Capabilities, Clarica

"Ambiguity and overload are the essence of every business day. *Simplicity* **offers a rational set of tools for leaders** to establish the clarity and connect people to choices and solutions. The idea that an elegant solution is in our abilities to listen, model behavior, and tell stories is powerful indeed."

> **D. LYNN MERCER,** Manufacturing & Global Provisioning Vice President, Lucent Technologies

"Bill Jensen demonstrates that truly **empowering employees**—providing them with the tools and capabilities required to thrive in today's increasingly complex and competitive environment—does not happen by chance. **It requires the conscientious investment of time and resources by senior management."**

> **HOWARD LEVINE,** Vice President, Business Consulting and Organization Development, Merck

"It is possible to simplify. With this book as your guide and instruction manual, you can make the complex clear. **Don't just read this book, keep it close at all times.** Refer to it, learn from it, rely on it. As Bill Jensen makes so clear: Simplicity is power."

> **WILLIAM LUTZ,** author of *The New Doublespeak: Why No One Knows What Anyone's Saying Anymore and Doublespeak Defined*

"*Simplicity* provides a very intriguing quest for meaning-making and more intelligent navigation around IC—(Intellectual Capital, as well as 'I See...Aha!'). **This book clarifies the huge hidden capabilities and potential in most enterprises.**"

> **LEIF EDVINSSON,** formerly Director of Intellectual Capital at Skandia now Global Knowledge Nomad and CEO of UNIC, Universal Networking of Intellectual Capital

"**Of many books that provide a 'real world' perspective of management thinking, *Simplicity* stands out.** Instead of adding to the soup of prevailing jargon, Bill Jensen captures the quintessence of the 'Discipline of Common Sense,' offering pragmatic perspectives on what to do and how to do it."

> **YOGESH MALHOTRA,** Chairman & CEO, @Brint.com L.L.C. Professor of E-Business & Knowledge Management

"As life has grown far more complex people have seized upon charming bits of design culture. We grab up Shaker boxes and Amish quilts like life preservers, as if merely by being near them we will absorb the wisdom of an earlier age and our lives will make sense. Now comes **Bill Jensen who does something far more valuable: He shows us explicitly how to clean up the mess, get more done, work better with others, and gain real control of our lives.** At last, Jensen gives us a useful prescription, not just a palliative."

> **LARRY KEELEY,** President, The Doblin Group

Simplicity

Simplicity

The New Competitive Advantage in a World
of More, Better, Faster

Bill Jensen

HarperCollinsBusiness

HarperCollins*Publishers*
77–85 Fulham Palace Road,
Hammersmith, London W6 8JB

www.harpercollinsbusiness.com

Published by HarperCollins*Publishers* 2000
1 3 5 7 9 8 6 4 2

A catalogue record for this book
is available from the British Library

ISBN 0 00 2571862

Set in Helvetica and Times

Printed and bound in Great Britain by
Caledonian International Book Manufacturing Ltd, Glasgow

To Mom

The hardest work is

figuring out what to do

in a world of infinite choices.

Making the complex clear
always helps people
work smarter.
Because it is a lot easier
to figure out what's important
and ignore what isn't.

Contents

This book is a tool for figuring out what to do in a world of infinite choices. Its goal is to drive new discussions about what it means to lead and work smarter.

HOW TO USE THIS BOOK

Simplicity is divided into four sections.

The front and the back of the book are designed to generate discussion about how we work now ("The Aha"), and how we might work in the future ("Simpler FutureWork").

The how-to stuff is in the middle two sections.
"Simpler WorkDays" describes what works now and can be used immediately.
"Simpler Companies" covers how you will have to change your infrastructure if you want to stay simple year after year.

Chapter 1 provides a one-page Framework for Getting Simple.

	THE AHA	SIMPLER WORKDAYS	SIMPLER COMPANIES	SIMPLER FUTUREWORK
Section	1	2	3	4
Simpler Disciplines		Compete on Clarity	Design Smarter Work	Lead Through Navigation
Chapters	1–3	4–8	9–13	14
Discover		The one thing you need to do and the tools to do it	The one thing your company must do and the strategy to do it	

The Simplicity Manifesto

Simplicity is power

The wealth creators change the rules.

Gary Hamel, strategist

In February 1994 the heads of Leadership Development at Nations-Bank, Jim Shanley and John Harris, gathered their team for an offsite meeting. The goal was to begin changing communication and connections between leadership, associate, and customer experiences in an organization that would later become one of the largest banks in the world.

At the end of the two-day session, the walls were covered with flip-chart pages, and there were many new aha's. Then came time for concluding remarks. John stood up, marker in hand....Picture the scene: John resembles the '70s TV character McCloud, a U.S. marshal transplanted from New Mexico. The show's plotlines revolved around how fuhgedaboudit New Yawkers continuously underestimated this country bumpkin. Similarly, John's aw-shucks style of probing belies how far he pushes with tough questions.

Marker in hand, John remarked, "So what we're saying is that"—he finished his thought by writing in big red letters—"SIMPLICITY IS POWER."

Seventeen letters. Three words that reenergized a quarter-century journey of my own, and—more important—compelled me to think about how far the prevailing wisdom had been pushed that day.

For about 400 years, it's been widely quoted that knowledge is power. Sorry, Sir Francis, it's time for an update. In today's info-saturated world, what you know is power *only if* you know how to use it to help you juggle the too many things that were all due yesterday. That kind of power is based on your ability to separate the important from the urgent. And that's based on how quickly you and your team can create meaning—figuring out which few factoids, bits, and bytes are critical from all the gazillions of pieces of information swirling around you—all that on a continuous, real-time basis.

Simplicity—the art of making the complex clear—can give us the power to get stuff done. Power to work smarter. It's a prerequisite if we want to leverage the untapped energy, innovation, creativity, and ideas that already exist in our organizations.

As an idea—before you have to do anything—simplicity is about power:

Simplicity is the power to do less (of what *doesn't* matter).

Simplicity is the power to do more (of what *does* matter).

But that power doesn't float into our laps. We've got to change some habits. Every day, you spend a lot of time figuring out what is important and what isn't. If you'd like to simplify your workday, there is one thing you need to do:

Use time differently. By changing how you organize and share what you know, you'll spend a lot less time on the things that don't matter and a lot more time on the things that do. When you spend more time making the complex clear, the figuring out part happens "for free."

If you'd like a simpler company, senior execs also must do one thing:

Work backwards from what people need. People will trust the corporate infrastructure to help them work smarter if tools, processes, and information are grounded in their needs. Simpler companies start where employees and customers meet, then work backwards into business needs.

Simplicity, like any other corporate discipline, is about the power to succeed. Unlike many other disciplines, if you want to create simpler ways of working, you can't tap-dance around the soft stuff. The very human issues of needs, trust, and freedom are constant, vocal traveling companions.

Gaining simplicity through clarity of ideas, instead of corporate edict, also challenges our assumptions about control. Business does control strategies, budgets, and much of the balance sheet. But when work is all about decision making, each of us controls—through the choices we make—what gets done and how we do it. This dynamic tension, even in our most "empowered" organizations, has yet to be fully explored. Simplicity happens when that tension gets attention.

Wealth creators change the rules. Therefore, this book has been designed for and dedicated to you—the organizational, project, and team leaders who are changing the rules of knowledge work. *Simplicity* is a leadership tool to help you help everyone to work smarter.

The Aha

1

What is your cost of confusion and the value of clarity?
Platitudes aside, our biggest limit is no longer the reach of our imagination. It's our ability to order, make sense of, and connect everything demanding our attention...how we create clarity.

Productive knowledge work is all about how we use each other's time and attention as we try to get stuff done. Your worst competitor is day-to-day confusion  —the time it takes everyone to figure out what to do and what not to do.

Before you worry about anything on the balance sheet, you need to consider: **1)** Are there enough people out there who can and will think their way through the confusion caused by leaders and companies who can't compete on clarity? **2)** What if your next-worst competitor — the one stealing your customers—gets simple first?

HOW DO I FIGURE OUT HOW TO GET STUFF DONE?

Simplicity

What it is and why it works

Simplicity is understanding of the whole.
It generates excitement. It's easy to view. Simplicity is timeless.

"Search for a Simpler Way" **study participant**

We've all experienced simplicity in our hearts, homes, and history. The utility of a perfectly balanced kitchen tool, the grace of Fred Astaire, the serenity of a Japanese garden, the pull of a Maya Angelou poem, the contours of an Eames chair, or the drama of humanity revealed in just 272 words in the Gettysburg Address. The simple elegance of these creations and talents ignites our imagination.

But how many of us have experienced the same kind of simplicity at work? What would a simpler workday or company feel like?

Think about yesterday. How did you spend your time? Like everyone else, you get only 24 x 7 x 52 hours per year. Are you spending enough of them doing your best and making a difference—because the clarity of the moment made it easy to figure out what to do and where to focus?

The Search for a Simpler Way

I witnessed a moment like that almost a quarter century ago. Ever since, I've been studying similar situations, trying to figure out how simplicity works.

I was a junior in college in upstate New York prepping for a midterm exam in logic. You know, if/then, and/or statements. Luckily, I had aced the same course in high school. We were even using the same textbook. So I was bored. I blew off the test and headed to Toronto with some friends to spend a few lost days.

While playing hooky, I stumbled upon the Ontario Science Centre.

It was filled with all sorts of cool interactive playthings, one of which was a maze with Ping-Pong balls poised above 12 channels. The objective was to get just one ball to drop to the bottom. The hard part was that each channel had gates that blocked the balls. To succeed, you had to figure out which levers would open which gates.

I watched two kids—fifth or sixth graders—try once, twice, and on the third attempt, they walked away high-fiving each other. Then it dawned on me. They weren't playing a game. They were performing college-level logic! By figuring out which gates would open by flipping only one lever (an "or" statement) and which channels needed two gates open (an "and" statement), these kids were taking the exam I had just skipped.

The maze designer had created a decision-making environment that stretched the users' thinking power, bringing out new levels of creativity and performance. And the kids had fun doing it.

The brilliance of the moment was an "elegant interface" (order through clarity and ease of use). The problem with thinking of it as a model for work simplicity is that it's linear. The world we live in is messy, full of contradictions. We are driven by competing priorities and emotions. Decisions rarely conform to a finite number of choices, flowing down predetermined paths with a limited number of levers to pull. Still, that experience led me to the study of clarity and how it can help us get things done.

Fast forward. During the late '80s and early '90s, I was helping companies go through change. Once the ten or so people at the top figured out a strategy, my job was to help translate it to the thousands who had to do the work.

I should say that's what I used to think was needed, and what I thought my role should be.

My beliefs started to shift about nine years ago. I was conducting focus groups for PepsiCo. We were introducing what was then the world's largest stock option plan. The plan's name, SharePower, reflected its goal—to reward hundreds of thousands of people for "thinking and acting like owners." The assumptions were the same as what you see in most any company: If we encourage and reward ownership behaviors, things will change. People will make better decisions, focused on customer and company success.

All the measures we took said people were getting it. The culture was growing and changing. Yet…something was missing. Even with all the "right" changes, many people asked, "Must all my choices, decisions, and work be so complicated? Frustrating? Difficult, confusing…inefficient?" And this was in a company that has created one of the world's finest leadership development disciplines!

During the next few years I noticed the same patterns *everywhere*— at highly successful companies and those struggling to survive, at big and little companies, and at the "most admired" companies, in boardrooms, back rooms, and at project meetings.

The Aha That Sparked Seven Years of Study

The universal problem seems to be how hard people have to work just to figure out what to do. Task work has been streamlined, but knowledge work has become more cluttered and confusing. Making the right choices—fast, while everything's changing—is now the toughest part of getting our work done.

I met with a few senior execs to share my beliefs that we could make it easier for people to figure out how to get their work done. Each struggled to contain his or her enthusiasm. "Stop trying to boil the ocean" or "cure world hunger," and…"Great in theory, but let's focus on the tasks at hand," as well as…"Been there, done that. We now have a HighPerformingFlexibleBuiltToLastBoundarylessLearning Organization."

Ever the optimistic masochist, I assumed that what they really meant was for me to work on the idea some more. So in 1992 I committed my firm to the "Search for a Simpler Way," a five-year study cosponsored by Northern Illinois University and focusing on Corporate America's ability to design work in the information age. We surveyed over 2,500 people, interviewing almost 1,000 of them.

We polled execs, managers, and line employees at companies like GE, Merck, Hewlett-Packard, Xerox, and Microsoft. Our research also included organizations that ranged from Kelly Services to the U.S. Army; from ServiceMaster to Avon, Domino's Pizza, America Online, Southwest Airlines, and Lucent. The final tally was over 460 organizations. The study stretched into seven years when we resampled the population in '98 and '99.

We asked people how they figured out what to do and how they got

CHAPTER PUNCHLINE

Simplicity works because it is based on human nature and common sense

THE JOURNEY BEHIND THIS BOOK

I stood on the shoulders of giants (see Acknowledgments, page 210), checked out the view, and reported what I saw. At the convergence of three disciplines—business design, communication design, learning design—I found another one hidden in plain sight: <u>The Discipline of Common Sense</u>

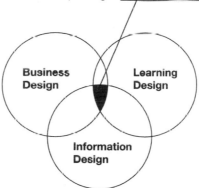

Creating clarity isn't new. Nor is the need for simplicity or the secrets of working smarter. Much of what you'll find in this book is common sense. Unfortunately, a lot of common sense basics seem to be uncommon, undisciplined, and unpracticed.

"Keeping things simple is profoundly misunderstood. If you begin by honoring the social mind, you engage in what I call cognitive judo. You let the world do more of the work for you. Follow that principle and things that were hopelessly complicated actually start to straighten out in a very interesting way."

JOHN SEELY BROWN, Chief Scientist, Xerox Corporation, Director of Xerox PARC

"Very often, people confuse simple with simplistic. The nuance is lost on most."

CLEMENT MOK
Chief Creative
Officer, Sapient

"We spend a lot of time studying how to make things simpler—how to make them user centered. It's important to be thoughtful about this. **Thoughtful enough** not to simplify things the usual way by throwing away all the complicated parts."

LARRY KEELEY, President, The Doblin Group

"This may be nothing new, but it's becoming extremely critical. More and more, as we move into this age of ambiguity and overload, there isn't a manager or leader anywhere who can figure it out alone."

BETH MIAKININ, Director Body Engineering, Saturn

"I believe there will be companies that get a jump on simplicity. And they'll have a huge competitive advantage when they do."

STEVE PLUMP
General Manager of UK
and Ireland, Eli Lilly

things done. What we wanted to know was this: With all that has changed in how we work, are we really working smarter, or just harder and faster?

Working Smarter: We're Still in Our Infancy

Here's a preview of the findings: Business is doing a great job at changing to meet marketplace, customer, and shareholder needs. And it is lousy at making work elegant—creating clarity of choice, then providing the tools and information people need to work smarter.

Business is getting real good at driving new choices into the organization. Yet it's in its infancy in figuring out how to connect people to those choices and how to leverage everyone's brainpower to make infinite use of finite resources and time. Top-performing companies do better than the rest, but they have only scratched the surface of what's possible and needed.

Here's a sampling of what we found:
From a manufacturing plant manager: "I've studied all 79 pages of the performance management training manual and still can't figure out what to do. Especially when I have to also implement [our reengineering program] as well as train all the drivers in new procedures."

From a mid-manager in a services company: "What's important to me is how to decide what to do....All the plans, spreadsheets and milestones...just tell me what's due when. I still don't have what I need that tells me how to get it done."

From an SVP of Finance, a manager in Ops, and a line worker in three different organizations came the exact same quote: "I know *what* I'm supposed to do to make these changes. I just can't figure out *how*."

The key findings of the study, as well as a website with more information, are detailed in Chapter 2.

The Right Kind of Order

We found that figuring out how to get everything done is really hard. Tougher than we care to admit.

In 1994 Peter Drucker, the father of modern management, nailed the challenge when he looked at the collective thinking and decision making of hundreds of millions of people and declared: "The productivity of knowledge work—still abysmally low—will become the economic challenge of the knowledge society."[1]

As he often does, Drucker then followed up by describing a path forward. In 1998 he declared: "The next information revolution asks, What is the MEANING of information and what is its PURPOSE? And this is leading rapidly to redefining the tasks to be done with the help of information, and with it, to redefining the institutions that do those tasks."[2]

Simplicity is an information revolution whose mission is to make the complex clear. It's about creating the "right kind" of order. Order that still encourages dynamic change, experimentation, the emergence of ideas, innovation, and learning. This order comes from the discipline of creating clarity and meaning for the people doing the work.

Why Simplicity Works

Gavin Kerr, a friend and an amazing person, clued me in to why simplicity works. He started his career in seminary then took a few turns through marketing, benefits, and HR. He was on a great track at Pepsi, but realized it would cost him more family and community time than he wanted to give. He's now head of transformation at University of Pennsylvania Health Systems.

During reengineering's heyday, Kerr headed a project called 10X for Pepsi New England. The company was shooting for improving four key processes by a factor of ten. He struggled with implementation as all the facets—strategy, systems, technology, budgets, etc.—grew more complex and interconnected.

One Friday I joined him on his long drive home. His family was still living in lower Connecticut while he spent five days a week just outside Boston. We talked for hours about 10X's implementation challenges, as well as successes and failures in our careers and what they all had in common. At one point, he said something so profound and elegant, it stuck with me: "People tolerate management's logic, but they act on their own conclusions."

Obvious, yes. But it's also profound because it says that human nature rules everything.

A weird shift happens when the companies we work for grow large enough (somewhere between three and fifty people) to formalize how things get done: We start believing that corporate logic— The Plan, The Process, The Whatever—actually governs the choices we make. We

"This is very important. Leaving clarity behind to get speed is abdication. As leaders, we've got to be clear and focused."

MATT KISSNER, CEO, Pitney Bowes Financial Services

"My guiding light has always been simplicity.
When I look at anything, I ask, 'How can we simplify this and put a smile on your face when you use it?'
This is the question I ask myself and my team every day."

BOB GLASS
Chief Technology Officer
Weaver Aerospace

"As I reflect back on all the breakthroughs I've seen, one thing was always present—unbelievable clarity. Not reduced to ducks and bunnies explanations...but the exciting, passionate clarity of an idea."

MIKE O'BRIEN, President
ZoomTown.com, Cincinnati
Bell's ASDL provider

"In a lot of people's minds, making the complex clear means you just dump information on everybody. That simply adds to the confusion."

NIGEL HOLMES of Explanation Graphics

"Most of life is simple and basic.
However, to keep it that way, we've got to get really good at thinking about thinking.
When I look at simplicity, I look at two things:
1) How we use language tools. They get you thinking.
2) How we ask questions. They get you thinking about the right things."

DON WINKLER, Chairman and CEO
Ford Motor Credit Company

even define *governance* as "how decisions get made."

Then, after we have spent gazillions of hours and dollars on that logic, we try to get the people doing the work to buy in to it. That is superinvesting in plans and underinvesting in how people really make choices. But human nature works the other way around. We *tolerate* the logic of things around us, but at the end of the day, what we *do* reflects the choices we make.

Simplicity works because it is based on human nature and common sense, not on corporate logic.

First: Start with the assumption that most people want to do the right thing and make a difference. Second: Recognize that we're living in a world of infinite choices, and that most people are truly struggling to figure out what will make the most difference. (Remember that even if you've created shared mindset, the human need to make one's own choices will play out every time.) Conclusion: Create order through clarity. Invest in how people really make choices.

But let's not be naïve. Simplicity is also about discipline. This book asks you, me, and the companies we work for, to grow out of our infancy in connecting people to choices. If we can make this change, everyone can work smarter, because knowledge work begins with our ability to order, make sense of, and understand everything that demands our attention.

Consider Before You Begin:
Simpler for Whom?

The paradox of simplicity is that making things simpler is hard work. If you are reading this book, you probably own that work. Simplicity could be the toughest job you never asked for but must take on.

Making things simpler doesn't have to be about more work for you, but it may mean working differently. The people you lead are seeking ideas and tools that will ignite their imagination, creating *just the right tension* between order and change. Isn't that what you crave, too?

Before you started thinking about simplicity, your job was already difficult. Leadership guru Warren Bennis says that your role as a leader is about creating the capacity to translate vision into reality. Think of simplicity as nothing more, or less, than self-sustaining feedback as you do that work. Make the complex clear and—for better *and* worse—accountabilities, trust, freedom, direction, and control become visible to

The Essence of Simplicity

ONE-PAGE SUMMARY

Simplicity always helps people work smarter

A FRAMEWORK FOR GETTING SIMPLE

COMPETE ON CLARITY	DESIGN SMARTER WORK	LEAD THROUGH NAVIGATION
Use time differently	Work backwards from what people need	Change the rules of the game
• Changing how time is used • Planning for conversations • Contracting for behaviors • Listening to ignore more • Engaging everyone	• Simpler to know • Feels simpler • Simpler to use • Simpler to do • Simpler to succeed	Structure your company according to the questions people ask

WHAT SUCCESS LOOKS LIKE

Simplicity is when time is organized for getting stuff done *and* thinking	Simplicity is when people can trust the company to help them work smarter	Simplicity is when companies are designed so people can navigate infinite choices
Create less clutter, or make sense of it faster, and you change how time gets used	When tools, processes, and information are grounded in what people need, execution is easier, faster, and smarter	The future is about the power of maps and structuring companies according to human nature

all. Make the complex clear and everyone can make a lot more decisions on his or her own—even while the world continues to create infinite choices.

Although I've tried to provide some tools and questions to jump-start your efforts, don't look for the dumbed-down "one-minute leader's guide to simplicity." It will never exist. Don't confuse "simplistic" with thoughtful design of how time and energy are used.

I haven't explored all the paths. I can claim only to have spent a number of years studying and talking to people about simpler ways of working. Mostly, I've recorded the challenges, confusion, and chaos felt by many, then relayed some of the ideas and people who are making waves.

I've tried to walk my own talk. I've tweaked the nose of my chosen profession—consulting jargon rarely simplifies. I've had fun with the topic. (Why get out of bed if getting stuff done isn't fun?) And I've tried to stick with "kitchen-table English"—how real people talk to each other. If I stumble, don't let my shortcomings deter you in your search for simpler ways of getting work done. This is too important. The best solutions have yet to be discovered.

Chapter 2

Simplicity's Evil Twin

How work got so complex

There comes a time in the affairs of man when he must
take the bull by the tail and face the situation.

WC Fields, vaudevillian and philosopher

In one sense, describing work complexity is a no-brainer. We feel it in
our bones. We're all too busy and haven't the time to attend to things.
For each of us, the urgent is constantly replacing the important.

But push Pause for just a moment. What do you think is causing that
complexity? The speed of change or its intensity? Technology or your
competitors? Managers not empowering others? Until a few years ago,
these culprits were at the top of my list. I promoted them in my role of
Corporate Shill—helping senior execs communicate change to their
troops.

About halfway through our "Search for a Simpler Way" study, new
patterns emerged. I began to understand what scientists are trying to
tell us about complexity. Even in chaos, when you study patterns, the
simplest of rules and solutions emerge. And myths are exposed for all
to see.

The Search

Throughout our study, we wanted to know how work really gets done
in the information age. We asked people how they understood what
they were supposed to do, how they decided how to do it, what tools
they used, and how they helped others know what to do.

To find out whether we're truly working smarter, or just harder
and faster, we asked: What will we find if we compare our systems
for getting work done—performance management, strategy
implementation, process designs, etc.—to how people *really* work?

My goal for this chapter is not to data-dump everything we found. For full in-depth analysis, we've built a companion website: http://www.simplerwork.com. There, you can download the entire 146-page study, examine study demographics with a complete listing of participants, as well as view additional readings and participate in chatspaces dedicated to simplicity.

In this chapter I'd like to use what I've learned to tell the story of how we work today. It may not be pretty. Or fun. But the tale is important because it can help us make sense of what frustrates our best efforts. And because it forces us to pause long enough to be thoughtful about how we can create simpler ways of working.

The Story of Work So Far

Heigh ho, heigh ho. It's off to work you go. You make choices. Lots of them. Some are according to The Plan, The Process, The Strategy, The Budget. Some are not. That's human nature. If there is any commonsense rule about how you work, it's that you will always make your own choices. Good or bad, efficient or not, within your company's definition of success or not.

Plot Twist: The "New Economy"—which changed work from making things to making choices—also changed the impact of each choice. Not only do you have to make more decisions, faster, but every decision is interconnected to the next one. More than ever, business success is tightly tied to the choices you make, and how you make them. For example: All the strategic planning in the world is worthless unless you understand the plan, buy in to it, and choose to use it to guide how you serve a customer.

Here's where the story veers from the script we all promote. While external forces such as customer needs, competition, and global markets definitely drive what needs to change and how fast, it's how we frame those choices and deliver information that creates the most complexity in our work.

Just when it is even more important that everyone make better choices, we find that business is lousy at making things clear. The top sources of complexity uncovered by the "Search for a Simpler Way" study are

- Lack of integration of change
- Unclear goals and objectives

• Ineffective communication

• Your knowledge management experience

(for a full list, see table on page 22).

Dirty Little Secret, Hidden in Plain Sight: Work complexity is the result of our worst intellectual habits. We're not structuring goals, communication, information, and knowledge so that a diverse workforce can use them to make decisions.

Unless we make some dramatic changes, the story of how we work is about the destruction of a cliché. Our biggest limit is no longer the reach of our imagination. It's now our inability to order, make sense of, and connect everything that demands our attention. We are failing to make the complex clear.

In reverse order, here's how the top four sources of work complexity affect you.

Why Do I Have That Sinking Feeling?

4 Imagine making a simple request: "I'd like a drink, please." Your Ministry of Water has the technology and solution to meet this very need. Suddenly, you're dropped in the middle of a vast saltwater ocean, thrashing to keep your head above the waves. Water, water everywhere, but not a drop to drink. For about three out of every four of us, this is what knowledge management feels like.

Your fourth biggest source of complexity is most likely how your company creates your **knowledge management experience**—what you go through to get what you need in order to work smarter. Useful info, knowledge, and wisdom are hidden within a sea of data. And the solution has little to do with technology.

This is not some Luddite's cry against progress. Consider the following numbers: 80, 60, 75, and 1,100. They represent the skills, needs, and personal filters people bring to this experience.

When we asked people about their ability to get and use what they needed to make quick and changing day-to-day decisions:

• 80 percent of front-line employees said they couldn't find what they needed or couldn't translate the available information into a decision

• 60 percent of the people with the titles of manager through senior vice president said the same thing

What Makes Work So Complex?

TOTAL STUDY UNIVERSE	MOST ADMIRED COMPANIES	TOP 75 PERFORMERS
2,509 individuals, including 955 interviews	16 of *Fortune's* 1997* 25 Most Admired Companies, 236 individuals, including 49 interviews	32 of *Business Week's* 1997* Top S&P Performers, 306 individuals, including 67 interviews
1 Integration of change	**1** Integration of change	**1** Integration of change
2 Unclear goals and objectives	**2** Knowledge management	**2** How we communicate
3 How we communicate	**3** How we communicate	**3** Knowledge management
4 Knowledge management	**4** Technology	**4** How we work as teams, with others
5 How we work as teams, with others	**5** How we work as teams, with others	**4** Technology (tie)
5 Technology (tie)	**5** Customer needs (tie)	**6** Customer needs
7 Our work processes	**7** Competition and market forces	**6** Our work processes (tie)
8 Customer needs	**8** Our work processes	**8** Competition and market forces
9 My manager's skills	**9** Human capital (Attracting/Retaining Best)	**8** Unclear goals and objectives (tie)
10 Competition and market forces	**10** Training, continuous learning	**10** Training, continuous learning

KEY

Lists indicate top 10 sources of work complexity—why people have to work so hard to work smarter. During each cut of the data, there was always a sharp drop in severity after the first three or four sources.

Note: "Unclear goals and objectives" does not appear on the Most Admired list, and is at the bottom of the Top Performers list.

* Follow-up resampling of these items in 1998 and 1999 showed no major shifts in the top four sources of work complexity.

Whoa! Sixty to 80 percent of us feel that the useful stuff must be there. Somewhere. We just can't find it or translate it quickly enough. In today's networked environment, how is that possible? At first, I didn't believe our own data. Then we compared our results to statistics about the population at large (mostly in the United States).

We studied Bureau of Labor Statistics data. Did you know that about 75 percent of the U.S. workforce lacks key literacy skills necessary to succeed today? When work involves the analysis, reasoning, and integration of "moderately complex prose, document and quantitative information," about three-quarters of us need additional tools and skills.[1]

This is no smart-or-dumb issue. It's about the need within our companies for appropriate design, tools, and expectations. Our findings also support the cries to replace the preplanned ways Corporate America uses to make change happen with constructive dialogue. Conversation can do the heavy lifting of knowledge work. It helps us make sense of everything coming at us.

In today's overloaded, complicated environment, three out of every four of us are focused on sense-making as Job One. Turning all the new information into action falls to a distant second. Yet much of today's knowledge management experience is like the infamous United Nations showdown with Soviet Prime Minister Nikita Khrushchev: "Don't wait for the translation, just answer the question!"

Then there's the raw tonnage of what's coming at you. We went ultraconservative. After tossing aside some Silicon Valley numbers:

• Twice as much, or more, info coming at us every year

and estimates from techno-gurus like George Gilder:

• Bandwidth tripling communication capacity every year for the next 25 years

the *most conservative estimates* we found show business information doubling every three years. That's twice as much information every 1,100 days.

Bottom line: At least every 1,100 days your ability to transform information into work becomes twice as important. Because, in that time, the amount of info you'll need to ignore, organize, translate, communicate, and build into solutions will double. (Imagine the impact if you consider the more aggressive estimates!)

Until knowledge management is truly user and needs centered, the experience is likely to remain a top source of complexity in your work.

Yack, Yack, Yack

3 As long as people are part of the process, we shouldn't be surprised by the importance of communication to getting things done. "Communication always sucks," bellows management gadfly Tom Peters. "It's very simple: It's the human condition....To make communication even halfway decent, even half the time, you've got to work like hell at it...all the time!"[2]

Peters' last point is a key explanation of why **ineffective communication** is your third biggest source of complexity. Everybody *thinks* they're working like hell at it. In reality, there's a lack of discipline behind most communication. Very few people know how to use it to do the heavy lifting we've already mentioned.

Over three-quarters of the senior managers we studied defined communication as the ability to deliver corporate messages so the workforce would focus on what's good for the company and the customer. Only 9 percent defined communication as sharing and using performance-based work information. When asked about this discrepancy, leaders cried, "That's managing, not communicating!" The workforce pushed back even louder, "You don't get it! That's clarity and making sense of everything. Because you don't see it that way, you put your emphasis on coordinating and things you can control—not on making things clear."

It's not that our leaders don't believe in the power and importance of communication. One hundred percent are there. The leadership gap is *how often* the urgent is replacing the important. Creating dialogue and connecting everyone to the Big Picture is important. Delivering the numbers is urgent. Based on leaders' current priorities, "managing" is Job One, and creating focus and understanding has fallen to a distant second.

But let's not lay this all at leadership's doorstep. Everyone else does most of the yacking in your company. All that day-to-day communication creates a lot of confusion. Here's a glimpse of what that looks like.

• About 80 percent of your internal communication—meetings, teleconferences, presentations, emails, etc.—consists of

- Sharing information that does not require action, and/or
- Communicating something for which there is no discernible consequence if the recipient ignores it

In other words, a lot of communication you thought was helpful may be seen as unfocused noise or just "FYI" junk mail by your teammates.

• Time pressure allows people to justify behaviors they would not accept from others. When people are *in need of* communication, they want others to take the time to listen, and then to take the time to create meaning, clarity, and connections between ideas. But when they have to *do the communicating*, saving time becomes a priority. Communication becomes a matter of disseminating information and taking any available e-shortcuts. When it comes to communication, business is facing major discipline and accountability problems. It's like the line about change: Taking the time to create clarity is important –as long as it's the other guy who has to do it.

• In our fast-paced environment, the lack of attention given to deep problem solving is being mislabeled. When study participants couldn't quickly identify a problem, *everything* —poorly designed processes, inadequate resourcing, supply chain hiccups, whatever—became a communication problem. Which makes the solution "Let's communicate more." But that just creates noise and distracts from the original problem. The best communicators know when to shut up and examine root causes.

    People—not programs, plans, or technologies—make the final choices about what to do and how to do it. Therefore communication that is designed for decision making is the linchpin of business success. The work behind it is a daily requirement for simplicity.

What Does Success Look Like?

2 I'm sure it's no surprise that in our study, top performers and "most admired" companies had very clear goals and objectives. And they worked very hard to keep them clear…day in, day out. Only rarely did any of the following issues apply to these top performers. Now for the painful part.

    If your company isn't among the absolute best of the best, the odds are good that your **goals and objectives are unclear** to most people in your organization. So unclear, in fact, that this is your number two source of work complexity.

Nothing here is brain surgery. Just really hard work. Every day. The greater the amount of change, the more work has to be put into ensuring that every individual knows what success looks like. Frankly, this discipline is lacking in most companies.

Lack of focus is one of the biggest, most obvious challenges. In complicated, changing environments, laser-sharp focus must be a given. Yet most study participants said their goals were unclear simply because there were too many of them. This overload is causing immense complexity. One company won our Dubious Distinction Award for trying to unite everyone around 136 "strategic" priorities!

Another major factor was lack of alignment of goals. With so many changes, it's really difficult for most of us to figure out how our goals connect to our coworkers', and how these goals add up to corporate success.

Unfortunately, Corporate America's solution to these problems seems to be perfecting the science of building strategic management systems. Study participants were looking for something different—the real basics. Two themes emerged that you've heard thousands of times before:

- Aligned goals and aligned leaders are, apparently, inseparable. Far too many organizations look well coordinated on paper but never address the politics at the senior-most levels. We seem to tolerate personal agendas at the top of our companies.
- True empowerment can be masked by a tightly structured approach to goal setting. "Our goals are clear at the enterprise level," said one director of organizational development. "But real clear goals at the line level means we'd have to create alignment through trust and communication. We're not ready to do that. We want to structure ourselves into alignment." Companies can actually use structured goal-setting activities to hide a lack of trust.

Given all the change rhetoric of the past two decades, we were surprised by the frequency and intensity of respondents' comments on senior alignment and company attempts to structure themselves into alignment.

Finally, lack of feedback is destroying whatever clarity companies do

60% to 80% INFO

of us can't find or translate the info we need for decisions

"Cognitive load theory describes
where things break down. When you're learning something
new and you're a novice, the load is extremely high.
There's a process going on in your brain called meta-cognition,
and there's just too much going on. You can't process it all.
So people try to simplify the demands of the situation through
negotiation—changing what's being asked of them."

DR. SUSAN LAND, Assistant Professor, Instructional Systems, Penn State

"I'm not pessimistic about this kind of complexity.

The human mind is amazing. But I'm only optimistic

to the extent that we get cracking.

This is a very big deal."

DR. MICHAEL O'BRIEN, psychologist, author of *Profit from Experience*

have. We found that many people start out with clear goals but quickly lose that clarity if they don't get regular and honest feedback. Performance reviews are not working. Most stink. (One survey by the Society for Human Resource Management found that 90 percent of appraisal systems are unsuccessful.)

If change is constant, feedback needs to be real-time and constant. For company and marketplace feedback, people need tools that communicate trends simply and provide helpful, easy-to-use information for making day-to-day decisions. To promote personal growth, feedback must come from continuous dialogue and coaching from teammates.

Again, you've heard these observations many times before. Will most businesses ever get serious about these basics? The best of the best already have.

The Number One Source of Work Complexity

1 "Sure, I know [my industry] is going through massive change. So what? What troubles me is that nobody at [my company] has interconnected how we change." This senior executive gave voice to a universal problem and the biggest source of work complexity, **lack of integration of change.**

He continued, "Our intranet content isn't linked to our quarterly projects, which aren't connected to our performance management system, which doesn't jibe with compensation design, which doesn't match our department goals, which aren't supported by training, which…you get the idea."

From a line worker in a manufacturing plant: "We're supposed to be Six Sigma-ing our way to ISO certification. Our team would blow management's socks off—if they would just make sure the training we get next week has something to do with the quality program they launched last year. And it would really help if our gain-sharing program had something to do with the way my team was managed."

From the head of organizational effectiveness at a *Fortune* 200 company: "We move from Hay to Broadbanding [compensation structures]. We put in 360° feedback. We do quarterly town meetings. We send our leaders and managers [for training at] CCL and Pecos River. We've matrixed reporting relationships. We've used McKinsey, Delta, ODR, and Andersen [consultants]. By itself, every single effort

What Is Integration?

Workforce View

Integration is the ability to bring together the information I need at one place at one time so I can make a decision that leads to success

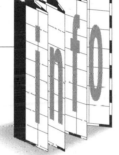

- Info access and availability
- Utility: Info is designed to match my needs and skills
- Quality: Info clarity and ease of use
- Efficient: Right amount at right time
- Effective: Designed to match decisions and choices I must make
- Info is connected and linked
- I am empowered to use what I find

Leadership View

Integration is the ability to bring together all the systems, structures, processes, people, capital, etc., so the organization can implement the strategic plan

- Mergers and acquisitions, joint ventures
- Aligned strategic plans and budgets
- Reporting structures, governance
- Alignment/teamwork among senior team
- Project management process
- IT: Merging acquisitions, legacy, and new
- Product or distribution channels
- Cross-selling/marketing
- Restructuring

is immensely valuable. But is any one of these things connected to the other? Uh-uh."

The number one source of work complexity today is that we expect integrated efforts from our workforce, but the infrastructure we're providing is smashed together.

To be fair, no organization or human being could figure out how to clean up and fully connect all of today's structures. Too much. Too fast. Too intricate. While the cleaning up and connecting shouldn't stop, you'll never plan your way into integration. The answer comes— surprise!—from our workforce.

Executives and the workforce see the challenge very differently:

• Senior execs define successful integration as the ability to bring together all the systems, processes, people, and capital so an organization can implement its strategic plan. These leaders are focused on the tools of governance, control, and coordination.

• The workforce defines successful integration as the ability to bring together "the information I need at one place, at one time, so I can make a decision that leads to success." The people doing the work are most focused on personal—not corporate-wide—tools for making choices. (For a full comparison, see table on page 29.)

Both views of successful integration are necessary and right. If senior execs don't focus on restructuring and everything else on their list, there would be no tomorrow for their organization. And if employees don't get what they need, implementation fails. It is critical to work equally hard on both sets of needs. But since leaders budget for and drive integration, guess which view gets short shrift?

Heigh ho, heigh ho. Corporate America is investing heavily in integrated planning and coordination. But it's chintzy when it comes to investing in human nature. We seem to ignore the fact that, as Gavin Kerr remarked, although people tolerate management's logic, they will always act on their own conclusions. Until we start thinking about integration as building the tools and information necessary for people to make personal choices, we are going to create a lot more work complexity than is necessary.

The Shock of How We Get Stuff Done

What do you find when you add together all four sources of complexity? "Future shock." I didn't realize it when we began, but we ended up studying a thirty-year-old concept of Alvin Toffler's. When he wrote *Future Shock*, Toffler spoke of a "frontal collision…that is now producing a decision-making crisis.…Taken together these pressures justify the term 'decisional overstimulation.' " He also called it "cognitive overload."

The symptoms go beyond mere information overload. We each have built-in coping mechanisms for that. We just shut down. Or we choose whom we'll listen to. Or we delete voicemails and emails en masse. But how does one cope with decisional overload? Where are the tools for navigating and choosing among infinite choices? Yes, there are success stories. No, they are not widespread.

Go back to the table on page 22. You'll notice that even in our best-performing and most admired companies, the top sources of work complexity all have to do with decision making and cognitive overload. (Not at the senior levels, but the closer we got to front-line employees, the more we saw future shock. It was worst for mid-managers.)

Understanding Toffler's insights changes how you listen. You begin to realize that resistance to change is often misdiagnosed. Large numbers of people—more than most of us care to admit—need new tools and skills if they are to work in a world filled with infinite choices. Yet because of our ability to think our way out of most any situation, we assume the difficulties along the way must be the result of people digging in their heels. Please, don't confuse choice overload with resistance to change.

It's All About Time

Alan Webber, editor of *Fast Company* magazine, says, "Most people aren't wandering around the streets, scratching their heads, thinking 'I'm hopelessly lost.' Most of the conversation is 'I love what I'm doing. I wouldn't trade it for anything in the world, but I am completely swamped. I'm overwhelmed by it all.' "

He's right. Very few of us talk about overdosing on choices. But we all have an inner sense of time. Our discussions are usually centered on how much we have to get done and how little time is available.

Unfortunately, such discussions are rarely balanced. We give the marketplace and technology too much credit for how little time we have. Lack of clarity within our organizations also robs us of major chunks of time.

CHAPTER PUNCHLINE

Lack of clarity is costing you dearly. It limits and contains people who are trying to work smarter.

"This is a critical productivity issue.

Work complexity may be *the* productivity issue for the coming decade. The obstacle, however, is not the ability or willingness of people to engage as fully committed knowledge workers. To seek, think, and create are human traits. The challenge is how management chooses to focus people's time and energy."

TOM PETZINGER, *Wall Street Journal* columnist, author of *The New Pioneers*

"People don't have the time, energy—and in some cases, the ability— to stay focused on just two or three very important things. Last year we had 167,000 new people in our organization. How the heck do you keep that kind of group centered? It's tough to do."

GARY BOSAK
VP of Transformation
Sears

"Often, senior managers are part of the problem. They actually think that what they say and what they design is the only information being disseminated. They don't understand how much churn is going on in their organization. So they reach to reorganizing, restructuring, and new processes. Because they don't understand why their people are confused, a lot of good people are getting injured by even more complexity."

JIM DIXON, head of Technology and Operations Bank of America

The head of a 20,000-person business unit quietly confided, "We're using people's time like it's a blank check." He was genuinely embarrassed. Corporate America is pushing a lot of unfocused decision making at you and calling it speed. Companies and leaders who are sloppy about clarity are confusing your personal time with business time.

Anyone preaching the elimination of corporate controls by pushing decision making down to front-line employees just doesn't get it. There is a new control game, and it's hidden in plain view. Michael Lewis, author of *Liar's Poker*, calls it "signaling one's place in the world: wasting other people's time without spending a moment of one's own."[3] Not one executive I've met plays this game intentionally. Most would sincerely be appalled if they realized what was happening. But study findings indicate too many companies have unknowingly exchanged one form of control for another.

Simplicity's paradox: Business must compete on speed *and* use your time effectively.

Hold the Elevator

In communication circles, there's the Elevator Speech. You've got to be able to get your key points across in the time you'd spend taking a short elevator ride. If you gave me just one ride and I had to tell you the story of what I learned over the past seven years, here's what I'd say:

- Confusion is costing you a lot more than you think. It *is* work complexity, and it's an abuse of people's time.
- Most people are extraordinary. They want to do the right thing and make a difference.
- If you want more people to make more of a difference (elevator doors open), you'll have to find new ways for them to create their own clarity.

If you wanted more as we walked down the hall, I'd close by saying:
- Creating clarity takes a little common sense and A LOT of discipline
- Both individuals and companies must be held accountable

Chapter 3

So What?

Does it hurt enough to do something about it?

Do, or do not. There is no "try."

Yoda, to Luke Skywalker

The story continues.... Simplicity is power. Work complexity is making everything too hard and confusing. More important, though, the lens through which we look at work has changed. The problem isn't something that happens to you from "out there." Your company and the people in and around it coauthor the top sources of complexity.

So what? Is that *your* problem?

Peeking through a new lens isn't enough to get you to take on the toughest job you never asked for. That will happen only when you believe the cost of confusion is greater than the work of getting simple.

WE'RE FOCUSED ON WHAT YOU NEED TO MAKE DECISIONS.

Leadership View

HOW DO I FIGURE OUT HOW TO GET STUFF DONE?

HOW DO I FIGURE OUT WHAT'S IMPORTANT?

HOW DO I NAVIGATE THROUGH ALL THIS ON MY OWN?

HOW DO I MAKE DECISIONS THAT LEAD TO SUCCESS?

Workforce View

Your first step is to think about what complexity is costing you: Emotionally, in terms of your bottom line, in lost opportunities for growth, in turnover among teammates, etc.

Two things will happen once you personalize the cost: (1) You will own part of the problem. Complexity will cease to be this shapeless fog that is someone else's job to fix. (2) You will begin to take back some control. Whenever something is important and urgent enough to warrant regular attention, it always seems to be more manageable.

That's where the following questions come in. They are designed to help you examine complexity in terms of day-to-day activities and your role in the company. A couple of the questions are softballs, lobbed to get things started. Some will feel like tough love. My goal is for at least one question to whipsaw your current conversation, and that the discussion will show you a way to get started.

The ideas and questions under the heading of "What would I change?" are focused on your role as an individual manager or a team or organizational leader. They will prepare you for Section 2, "Simpler WorkDays," where you will be asked to use time differently. You will likely find that the conversations started in this chapter will flow right into that section.

"What must we change?" is mostly for senior execs with business unit or corporate-wide responsibilities. The questions under this heading address complexity issues that must be fixed with infrastructure, tool, and process design. Section 3, "Simpler Companies," will ask you to rethink those things—working backwards from what people need. Human nature being what it is, you will only create that much work for yourself if you believe that living with your present complexity will hurt more and cost you more.

What Would I Change?

The Conversation Starter: Two Pictures Worth Zillions of Words
Go back to the funnel and dots. They are a graphic representation of what we found during our study. I had buried them among the findings—until I saw people's reactions to them.

Photocopy the two pages together and ask a dozen or so people in your organization if the images are at all relevant to them. Watch their pupils dilate and their necks and hands come to life. Listen to their reactions. Their comments will point to immediate places where you can start dealing with complexity. While few will admit "this is how I bury people in dots," most can give you a rapid-fire list of what is causing the dots they have to hack through.

Is It Time to Call a Headhunter?
Close the door. Sit alone for a few minutes. Think deeply about how your company, team, or department uses *your* time. What conclusions do you come to? Be fair. How much of that could you change? How much of the time drain is truly "just the way things are," and how much is a serious abuse of your time on this earth?

According to a 1998 Yankelovich survey, one in three adults said they'd accept a smaller paycheck in exchange for a simpler lifestyle. Would you jump ship for little or no gain if your firm's competitor put simplicity on the table?

Now imagine your direct reports or immediate teammates getting the same offer. How many would jump? If you don't like the answer, think back to the top sources of work complexity we discussed in Chapter 2. Among them are unclear goals, ineffective communication, and poor knowledge management. As a leader or manager, how much of that could you remedy?

Is Complexity Causing Problems You Hadn't Looked For?
After they defined complexity, we asked people if they had experienced more, less, or the same amount of complexity over the past three years. More than half said that complexity at work had increased significantly. Of those people, one out of every six said that the complexity had increased "more than I can successfully manage." These individuals

were in choice overload and found it really hard to pick the important stuff out of all the dots. Has your business grown significantly more complex? If so, who are among your one in six? Are they affecting customer service? How others are managed? New product development? When you know the answer you can target where simplicity would have high impact on the business.

What Must We Change?

Would You Like to Cut Costs or Grow More?

In a recent survey by Bain and Company, almost half the top execs interviewed said cost-cutting was a key strategy for ensuring success during times of uncertainty.

If, as our study indicated, work complexity is wasting up to two hours per day per person, finding ways to get those two hours back is really important. Reducing complexity is like headcount reduction for free. You can reduce costs without losing a single person. Or, if your focus is top-line growth, you can gain up to 120 minutes per person per day for new ideas and innovation.

If you look at just the United States, where around 134,000,000 people are employed and earn an average wage of $13.29/hour, those wasted two hours add up to big bucks![1]

The following table shows the costs of cognitive overload in the U.S. While it wouldn't hold up in a cause-and-effect debate, the data in the

COGNITIVE OVERLOAD: A $1.3 TRILLION U.S. INDUSTRY?

Work complexity's drain on the economy: **Between $890 - $926 billion**[1]
The cost of stress-related problems: **At least $200 billion**[2]
Business' tab for *remedial* education: **$40 billion**[3]
Yearly fees for management consulting: **$113 billion**[4]

Sources: 1. Search for Simpler Way/BLS data combined 2. American Institute of Stress
3. Gary Huggins of Education Leaders Council 4. Kennedy Research Group 1999 projection for 2000

table is a proven tool for getting an executive's attention. Change the scale of the numbers and the data can serve as a corporate snapshot. Is anyone on your senior team tracking the costs of cognitive overload? Do those same execs have strategies for cutting expenses or booking revenues by providing what people need to overcome overload?

Do You Have a Critical Mass of Leaders?

Watson Wyatt recently surveyed over 2,000 executives around the world and concluded that leadership development is the top HR issue facing companies today. The American Society of Training and Development cites the lack of adequate succession planning as the most pressing need within leadership development—and we haven't even considered the impact of complexity on our leaders.

If work complexity continues to grow, what additional burdens will be placed on tomorrow's leaders? Do you have the leaders "in the pipeline" who can manage a decision-making environment that is on cognitive overload?

On the flip side: Could tackling simplicity be the ultimate development opportunity? That is, would selecting key execs to work on simplicity now not only feed the pipeline but also create a simpler company?

Is There a Critical Mass to Follow How You're Leading?

Are there enough people out there who *can* and *will* think their way through the complexity inside your company? Whether they work individually or in teams, are there enough loyal brainiacs in your employment pool who love dealing with lack of integration, unclear goals, and the other sources of complexity?

You are facing a choice. Either get simple—fast—or bet that you will always be able to find people who can and will think through whatever half-built stuff you throw at them. The latter may be a viable strategy. If that's your bet, consider the following costs of getting and keeping the people who will outthink complexity for you:

- **Hiring:** In 1998, Andersen Consulting culled through 3,000,000 resumes and 200,000 first interviews to field 15,000 new hires. While your scope may be smaller, you can't afford for your search to be any less Herculean.
- **Pay:** iQuantic is a San Francisco-based firm that tracks Silicon

Valley equity practices. Their studies show the median annual stock grant for customer service reps is 300 shares. Mid-managers get about 1,000, and top sales people get up to 19,000 shares—every year. It doesn't matter if you're not competing with these firms. Pony up similar amounts of equity or lose the talent to a company that will.

- **Education and Training:** You'll need to search the globe aggressively for talent. According to the Center for Educational Reform:
  - February 1998 math scores show American high school seniors outperforming only 2 of 21 nations and finishing significantly below 14 of those countries
  - In science, the United States is well below 11 countries, scoring ahead of only 2
- **Power and Control:** You're working hard at creating new ways of organizing human effort and creativity. Is it enough? In 1999 Tom Petzinger of the *Wall Street Journal* reported on the Cluetrain Manifesto (www.cluetrain.com). The manifesto's authors wanted Corporate America to "get a clue" and "take...million[s] of us as seriously as you take one reporter from the *WSJ*. We have the real power and we know it. If you don't impress us, your investors are going to take a bath. Don't they understand this?" Too in-your-face? Possibly. Based on real views that are gonna bite you in the butt? Quite probably. Consider the Cluetrain carefully. It may the warning shot of what's to come from 80 million *new* workers and managers (see Net Geners, in Chapter 10).

Can you afford *not* to rethink how everyone in your organization figures out what's important and navigates among infinite choices?

The Cost of Confusion

I haven't walked a mile in your shoes. I don't have the answers to these issues in your company. I can offer only what I've learned by asking dumb questions like these.

What I have learned is that for *all* firms competing on ideas, knowledge, and people, the universal context is the illustration on page 35. The "dots" around us are infinite choices swirling within a tsunami of data and info. This is the context in which *every* conversation about customers, employees, vendors, partners, and competitors takes place.

CHAPTER PUNCHLINE

Doing the work to get simple…

If not you, who?

CAN WE SOLVE COMPLEXITY WITH TEAMWORK?

Not the way most teams function. McKinsey & Company director Jon Katzenbach has written extensively on the power of teams. Successful teams, he says, need to:

- Be clear about their purpose, believing it's important
- Know their specific goals
- Know how they'll accomplish their goals
- Have the right set of skills for their team
- Hold themselves accountable for results

Compare these requirements to the top sources of work complexity we have already discussed. You'll find that many of your teams are jumping into knowledge work without clarity. They quickly create their own decisional overload and complexity, which affect others.

CAN WE SOLVE COMPLEXITY WITH TECHNOLOGY?

"Technology can create exciting opportunities. It also overwhelms us with choices."

PAUL SAFFO

Institute for the Future

"Digital networks ride on top of social networks, rather than replacing them. Without the trust, reciprocity, and community that the social network provides, a digital pipeline of virtually unlimited bandwidth will be useless."

FRANCIS FUKUYAMA, in *Trust: The Social Virtues and the Creation of Prosperity*

Simpler WorkDays

Are you using clarity to go faster, work smarter? Your company is 50 percent accountable for creating clarity. Guess who owns the other half? This section is about the passion and personal mastery required for you to **compete on clarity.** The people we choose for our teams, as well as the leaders we choose to follow, will increasingly create the power to get stuff done by making the complex clear.

Every chapter in this section focuses on the one thing you need to do if you are going to compete on clarity: **Use time differently.** You can do it by changing how you organize and share what you know— understanding what other people need to work smarter, then changing how you communicate is the grunt work of simplicity.

Each chapter in this section focuses on what **works now—the models and tools** you'll need to use time differently. You will discover how to design communication time for getting stuff done <u>and</u> thinking.

Success is easy to recognize. When you bring discipline to creating clarity, at first you'll free up a few more seconds. Then minutes. Then hours. That time is then available for figuring out what to do or what not to do. Each workday becomes a little simpler when you create less clutter for others, and make sense of it faster for yourself.

GETTING STARTED

Each chapter in this section builds upon the previous one. But jump in anywhere. The models and tools can be used independently and immediately.

SIMPLE NOTES

You will find that each chapter can be read from different perspectives: doer, team member, or leader—even parent or community member. There is no wrong perspective. Changing how you use time applies to all of your roles.

Chapter 4

Using Time

Getting ready to use people's time and attention

First learn the meaning of what you say, and only then speak.

Epictetus, Greek Stoic philosopher in Rome

Fact: Leaders get things done through other people. Unfortunate Fact: Most leaders are failing to get people focused on the right things. Result: Time and attention are often spent on nonessential, non-value-added activities.

For many of us, that's the picture of an average day. We also have extraordinary days—where every second and all of our attention is focused on the right thing at the right time. Magic happens, and the leaders around us contribute to that moment. What is the difference between an average and an extraordinary moment?

Think of the great leaders you know. Include great teachers and coaches too. All of them have at least one thing in common: It's how they use our time that makes them special. They take face time and make it valuable on multiple levels. Given just minutes, they affect our heads, hearts, and—through focusing and asking the right questions— what we do. They deliver more value in a shorter period of time, more bang for our minute.

Competing on clarity means creating that kind of value. More often. More consistently. It means organizing your ideas, questions, and information in ways so others can make sense of things faster. That means both you and those around you free up just a few more seconds or minutes to reflect, question, and learn before jumping into action. In the process, you change how knowledge work gets done.

For example: Cathy Carmody cherishes her years at Monsanto because CEO Bob Shapiro is so focused on helping people make sense of things faster. "Shapiro believes that the company's competitive advantage is how we relate to each other," says Carmody.

Her role as change agent has been to help Monsanto work smarter by using time for getting stuff done and thinking. "A lot of my work is just helping leaders and managers ask questions they didn't ask yesterday. Those questions change their focus, which ends up changing the work they do faster than any planning process. And, depending on the size of the business unit, changing the work of those leaders today means saving time for hundreds or thousands of employees tomorrow. Knowing what people need to make decisions and helping them make sense of things can have a huge impact on how time is used throughout a company."

Delivering More Bang for Everyone's Minute

On the eve of his retirement, Mel Goodes was reflective about how he had spent his time and what that meant. "When I took over as chairman, people said Warner-Lambert was among the walking dead in the pharmaceutical industry." Years later, Goodes was leaving at the top of his game. Under his leadership, the company's market value had grown from $9 billion to almost $60 billion—an increase of more than 500 percent in just over seven years.

"I like to think I train people," Goodes continued. "I believe in and expect performance. But I also believe people need to be motivated and developed. Right after I announced I was leaving, my wife found me sitting alone in the living room. She asked, 'What are you doing?' …'Crying.'…I was reading fifty or sixty letters from people who wrote to say thanks. It was emotional. It moved me."

Goodes insists that the letters and the improvement in the company's performance were the direct result of how he spent time with those around him. "All of us in the office of the chairman have been mentoring people for years. Whenever I go into new situations, the first thing I ask is, 'What would you like me to see?…Show me whatever you think is important.' Why should anyone work 40, 50, 60, 70 hours a week if they didn't like what they are doing and think it is important?"

Goodes believes that the link between investing time in people's development and finding simpler ways of working is universal: "Look at Jack Welch. Doesn't he talk about simplicity? Here's a thing about him that hardly anyone knows. We hired two people from GE about ten years ago. I recently saw Jack, and the first thing he says to me is…'How are those two doing?' He names them. They left GE 10 years ago! And they weren't top, senior people. As CEO, he's tough. But he also shows a concern for people. He invests time in them and wants to see them do well. I think that's an important value."

Dave Browne is CEO of LensCrafters and co-CEO of its parent company, Luxottica. He thinks a lot about getting ready to use associates' time. Even when *his* nights are sleepless. (When he shared the following, Browne mentioned that the past two weeks were filled with 20-plus-hour days. Luxottica was in the homestretch of acquiring Ray-Ban.)

"We have a very disciplined system for organizing and prioritizing everything that goes to our LensCrafters stores," says Browne. "We don't have a LensCrafters headquarters. We have a Cincinnati Service Center. We're here to serve the stores. We make the store managers' lives as easy as possible for their primary mission, which is to serve customers. Part of how we add value is to sort and prioritize all the stuff that goes to stores. Big programs, directives, initiatives, all go through a disciplined process before going into the weekly store package."

These leaders, and their competitive situations, are different. But they, like the great leaders you know, all make the best use of time. Sometimes they focus on the "soft" stuff, then connect it to the "hard." Sometimes they just ask better questions. Sometimes they focus on tools and processes that deliver what we need to make the best choices. All approaches work, because, as you will see, these leaders have relied upon some basic building blocks.

First: A Wake-up Call

Delivering more bang for everyone's minute isn't just a nice to do or the coddling of others. It is an essential part of working in the *Attention Economy*. More than ever, to deliver business results, you need people to volunteer their time and focus their attention on what you think is important. Yet choice overload is creating an opposing force. Self-preservation demands that we tune out a lot of what comes at us. This means that every project, every request, comes down to bartering for people's time and attention. (See sidebar on page 51.)

Unfortunately, many of us assume too much. Often we believe that we are well prepared to use other people's time and attention: "We all understand the company mission, we live by the values, we know what the goal is—let's go! Let's get started!" My mom had an expression for this mistake. She used to say, "You know what happens when you assume, don't you? You make an ass of u and me."

The Building Blocks for Using People's Time

If you would like to stop assuming, there are five building blocks you need to use every time you set out to grab a minute, or an hour, of someone's time and attention: Know, Feel, Use, Do, and Succeed.

If your goal is to create a simpler workday, the importance of these five building blocks cannot be overemphasized. When you use the building blocks people will be more likely to let you use their time, but if you are unclear on any of the five, you will find that a lot of *your* time will be spent looping back to re-communicate and clarify what you really meant.

KNOW	FEEL	USE	DO	SUCCEED
Knowing which few things are important	Considering and planning what the experience will feel like	Focusing on the tools and resources to be used	Creating and managing expectations	Creating a teachable view of what you are trying to achieve

Most often, the building blocks aren't difficult. But they do require getting disciplined about clarity. Working through these building blocks (pages 52-61), will help you create simpler workdays because:

• They shift your thinking

Most of us believe that we are being clear most of the time. Most of us are not. Run through the five building blocks before you launch any project and you'll quickly learn whether you're about to compete on clarity or confusion.

• They help you focus and leverage everything you've already got.

Business has made amazing progress in delivering results through disciplined collaboration. Teams, knowledge management, organizational learning, communities of practice, and mentoring are just a sampling of ways companies help people connect with each other. Even if you never gave it much thought, the five building blocks are behind every successful collaboration. Formalize how you think about them and you will always show up with something worth sharing and a clear way of doing so.

• You will use the raw materials over and over

Think of the five building blocks as musical notes. Once you know the notes, you can play them in infinite ways. Know, Feel, Use, Do, and Succeed can be shaped into new tools and models for:

- Changing how you plan (Chapter 5)
- Changing how you contract with teammates (Chapter 6)
- Changing how you listen and scan everything that comes your way (Chapter 7)
- Changing which details to use in strategic stories (Chapter 8)

Most Important Takeaway from This Chapter

Self-evaluation. How often are you ready—really—to use people's time and attention? Are you assigning projects and coordinating teams using three or fewer of the building blocks? For example, during our study we found that many teams were operating with unclear definitions of success, were clueless about the broad array of tools and resources that were available, and couldn't articulate the two or three things that would have the largest impact on their project's outcome.

The leaders, managers, and firms mentioned in this book are doing better, but they're not perfect. The five building blocks are the daily, nitty-gritty details people need in order to make choices. Yet very few companies—almost none—are consistently and continuously clear on all five. If you go through the rest of this book knowing which of the five you need to work on, you will have already begun to compete on clarity and to change how you use time.

CHAPTER PUNCHLINE

There are five building blocks for working smarter.

Creating clarity on each changes how you use time.

THEORY CORNER
COMPETING ON CLARITY
IN THE ATTENTION ECONOMY

The new marketplace is based on a simple idea: Although information is essentially infinite, demand for it is limited by the number of waking hours in a human day. How you use people's time—(e.g., the context and tools you provide)—has become the key driver of how they'll focus their attention. You must know why people will spend their time and attention on you.

Among the tenets:
- Using time and attention is a zero-sum game. No matter how good you are at multitasking, you're reading only these words now. When one thing—an initiative/change/whatever—gets attention, something else is denied.
- Attention is rich and complex because it comes in many forms: Commitment of time, recognition, guidance, obedience, thoughtfulness, caring, assistance in new skills, etc.
- Attention can't be bought. In the same way that advertising doesn't guarantee consumers will pay attention...all your compensation schemes, budgeting allocations, and reporting structures cannot guarantee that associates will pay attention.
- One of the biggest downsides: The increasing demand for attention and limited time can keep us from thinking deeply and enjoying the moment.

Michael Goldhaber, Howard Rheingold, John Browning, Spencer Reiss, *Wired* magazine

Know

What: Know which few things are important

Why: Everyone needs clarity on what will make the most difference

Because: You probably haven't thought enough about what you're about to ask others to do. If you're going to use their time, you need to answer "What are the three or four things I want people to know, understand, learn, or question?"

Kent Greenes is chief knowledge officer for SAIC, a San Diego-based high-tech research and engineering firm. During his previous stint at BP Amoco, Greenes and his team saved and added almost $700 million to the bottom line. He believes in the power of "getting clear about what is important. The ability for someone to make a decision and do the right thing involves lots of stuff. We work hard at simplifying three points in every process to get that kind of clarity. For us, knowledge management is simply learning before, learning during, and learning after whatever it is you're doing."

"We get people focused through one-page tools," Greenes continued. "If you can actually get everything on one page—and not just editing stuff out—that means the tool and the process caused you to reflect on what it is you want to do. Part of my job is to create the time and space to think. And if you limit the number of pages people have to explain themselves, it forces them to reflect first and think about what they're

SIMPLE NOTES: KNOW

- Clarity is not about faster access to more info.
  Nor does it involve packaging and marketing change.
  Clarity is about creating the space and time to think.
  Making it easier to ask new and better questions.
- Creating clarity and focusing attention on a few things
  is about taking risks. It's much easier and safer for you
  to throw a lot of stuff at the wall and see what sticks.
- Don't confuse clarity and certainty.
  Clarity is understanding enough to manage oneself.
  Certainty is buying into the illusion of control
  offered by plans and strategies.
- Many companies try to substitute "frameworks for
  thinking" for details. These include Mission, Vision,
  Values, and Principles. Done well, the substitution
  can work. Unfortunately, many frameworks are only
  plaques on the wall. Too few firms have built the tools,
  training, and management processes or spent the time
  to ensure that these things guide daily decision making.
  Those that have are the top performers and the most
  admired companies.

trying to do. That's very important."

"A lot of our knowledge program is about making it easier to reflect and easier to find the people who know something who might help you." Even with that support, Greencs says, getting clear about what it is you want to do takes work. "After every project we do what the U.S. Army calls an After Action Review. We ask: (1) What was supposed to happen? (2) What did happen? (3) Why are they different? If there were problems, invariably they happen when people started without enough time or thought on the first question."

Feel

What: Consider and plan for what the experience will feel like.

Why: No one makes decisions without feelings.

Because: The process of figuring out what to do always has emotions attached to it. Getting ready to use people's time means answering the question, "How do I want people to feel? And is that realistic based on what they're learning?"

"I must admit, I was completely blind to it before," says Steve Plump. Before returning to the United States recently, Plump spent several years as Eli Lilly's general manager for the United Kingdom and Ireland. He generously shared a lesson learned about the importance of thinking through what an experience will feel like.

"I was in a European business plan meeting. We had the strategy and measures in place, and the senior team was completely aligned. In one of our market segments, the country manager had done everything we had asked—he had built terrific market share. But our new strategy called for sales and profitability to be the focus instead of market share. So in front of him we said, 'This business isn't very profitable. Long term, should we even be in this business?' By the time he left, he thought we were all lunatics."

Plump continued, "I kept thinking, 'Geez, what did we do to this guy?' He comes in thinking he's the hero of all heroes because he's

SIMPLE NOTES: FEEL

- Deal with experiences well, and you get to go faster. Blow it, and you'll revisit decisions again and again. Clarity, attention, and feelings are joined at the hip. That's human nature.
- "Respect" in the Attention Economy means thinking through how and why someone else would buy in to your conclusions and beliefs.
- Skill-building: Author Daniel Goleman calls the required skills emotional intelligence. You may call it self-awareness, empathy, persuasion, managing relationships, reading people's feelings. They are all part of working in team-based, collaborative environments.

built a business from zero to around 40 percent market share, then he leaves feeling like he got nailed. And then…we decide to stick with the business anyway. What did we do to morale when he goes back? We just didn't think about the experience we created with that discussion."

"I firmly believe that leadership's role is to create experiences and beliefs," concluded Plump. "But most of the time, I had been focused on big moments or our 'culture.' It's really the little moments and everyday conversations that create or destroy what people feel. Until that moment, I was blind to the fact that our operations committee had done the planning necessary for Eli Lilly to succeed—but we hadn't thought through the experience of connecting people to that plan. It's so powerful once you see it."

Use

What: Focus on the tools and resources that are to be used.

Why: This is how people get the work done.

Because: Even with a shared vision, more employees than you may care to admit don't have the tools or training to do what is expected of them.*

Clarity about the use of tools and adequate levels of training is critical. But clarity comes second. Investing in the tools comes first.

Wendy Dixon is a marketing vice president, responsible for all of Merck's new products in the United States. She feels blessed with the ability to read fast and grab the essence of things. But she also knows that for many "the hard work of making sense of things is immensely difficult with data constantly coming at you. We are working in an industry with multiple customers and stakeholders (including patients, physicians, payers, regulators, etc.). Add to that complex channels, world-class competition, and data-driven marketing, and the challenge grows. We need to provide people in our organization with the tools to help them sort through the information and get to the salient issues and opportunities."

That's why Dixon is thrilled about the toolkits and training that Merck has built. "We developed a specific set of marketing principles,

SIMPLE NOTES: USE

- A recent Watson Wyatt survey of 9,144 American workers found that 57 percent[*] said they didn't have the tools, training, or information they needed to help meet company goals.

- Most tools are underused and misunderstood— usually because several of the building blocks— Know, Feel, Use, Do, and Succeed—were poorly communicated.

- Tools don't have to cost oodles of money. Tools for knowledge work include anything that clarifies, focuses, organizes, and delivers information. Any gathering or technology that connects people is also a knowledge work tool.

- This building block helps people figure out how they will get everything done. The others—Know, Feel, Do, and Succeed—help them to focus on what is important, and to sidestep what isn't.

a framework on how to go about top-class marketing. We wanted to help people think about the information coming at them. How to ask certain questions. How to choose what to focus on and what not to. We then took the principles and developed a series of tools to provide methodology for answering the questions, together with mechanisms to ensure rapid response. The end goal was to be able to quickly identify and answer the right questions, and then act accordingly. Looking back at the tools' first year of use on selected products, what you see is…bam, bam, bam…the tools lined up decisions. People could work a lot smarter within the core principles."

Dixon added, "We have the principles and the tools. Now we're putting in place systematic training so that every person in the company who does marketing can use them."

Do

---

What: Create and manage expectations.

Why: It is essential to be clear about the process and the next steps.

Because: When "command and control" became a bad thing, many managers lost the ability to be clear. People still need to know what to do. Only now that means understanding steps in a process. It means letting everyone know who will be doing what and when.

"We successfully created a culture of sharing, but we didn't necessarily have the right people talking to each other," observes Mark Koskiniemi, VP of Human Resources for Buckman Labs—an organization applauded for its knowledge management practices. "We had good cross-functional communication, but there was precious little going on at the manager-to-associate level. We just weren't clear about our expectations in this area."

"We developed software that makes the steps in this kind of dialogue explicit," Koskiniemi continued. "We have what we call triggers. Let's say somebody moves into a new position or we decide to move out of a market. Those would be triggers to say, 'Hey, it's time for us to look at your role in the organization. Let's go through the profiling process again and make sure we're all in alignment.'"

SIMPLE NOTES: DO

- Look for what Koskiniemi calls triggers—changes that would change what is expected of someone. Identify them for each project. Attach expectations to them.
- People have far too many things to do. Far too many triggers to think about. They appreciate and will use anything that organizes next steps.
- Fast-track and developing projects—where workflow and dynamics constantly shift—require a very strong team leader who regularly does "expectation check-ins."
- Add another dimension to "respect" in the Attention Economy: Crystal clarity of expectations.

Getting clear and managing expectations can also be low-tech. Bank of America is currently training over 170,000 people to better understand market forces and the bank's strategies. Leaders' Toolkits were prepared in which there are four bullets under the heading of "What Should Leaders Do?" Among those actions listed are "Engage your associates in a dialogue about what they've learned and what it means to be in their role." Associate takeaways also identified what they could do after the session to continue to build on what they had learned.

Succeed

What: Create a teachable view of what you're trying to achieve.

Why: People define success differently than businesses do. It is a lot easier to understand what success looks like if you include behaviors.

Because: People start far too many projects without knowing what success looks like. Along with Business Results and Project Milestones, people need to know how success will change how they and their teammates interact—how they spend their time and attention.

As a plant manager for Lucent Technologies, Lynn Mercer is not shy about tracking the usual measures of success. "Each week, we print projects on big sheets of paper and cover them with red, yellow, and green magnets. Just like a traffic light: Green means go, yellow means caution, and red…there's a problem. If the magnets are all green, I don't even ask questions."

"Each month, we track 10 different dimensions of success on a matrix. I'm able to compare the past three years to how we're currently doing on product, dollars of output productivity, manufacturing

---

SIMPLE NOTES: SUCCEED

- Any definition of success must have three measures:
  Results, Milestones, and What Successful Behaviors
  Will Look Like.
- *Behavior* just means what you would see or hear if
  people were walking the talk.
- For fast-track or developing projects, you may not need
  to be superexplicit—a conversation and a quick agreement
  among teammates will do. But if new members join the team,
  you must make the definition of success more explicit.
  Never bring in new teammates or hand off responsibilities
  to them without going over the three measures of success.
- A clean handoff on all three measures should take less
  than two minutes.
- Until your team is disciplined, ask "What's our definition
  of success?" at least once every meeting.

---

inventory, and several other measures," says Mercer. The tight tracking is possible because every August, she and her team go offsite and create the "10 vital few" matrix.

Mercer also makes sure that success is spelled out clearly enough so that people can know whether or not they're managing themselves and growing, and what successful behaviors look like. "When people come in here from any other culture, they learn that reaching a mediocre goal is less meaningful than setting a hard one and not hitting it. We spend a lot of time training everyone so they know what ownership accountability looks like. We make sure everyone is relentless in asking, 'Am I figuring out what is important and doing what's right?' And for managers the question is 'Am I letting others do what's right and important?' True success comes when you hit a crisis or rough spot, and people don't revert to old behaviors. That's the real hard part for all of us."

Chapter 5

Planning

The starter kit for simpler work

A child of five would understand this. Send someone to fetch a child of five.

Groucho Marx, keen observer of planning as usual

We all do a lot of planning. Big plans, like how the business will make or spend millions. And little plans, like scheduling the next team meeting. Yet what exactly does a plan do?

By itself, absolutely nothing. A plan is nothing more, or less, than a tool to have a conversation. The most critical factor in the success or failure of any plan is whether or not the conversation changed or coordinated what people do. A plan is a tool that helps you:

- Focus people's attention—from infinite choices to a short list of things to do
- Communicate what is important and how it will be measured
- Communicate daily priorities
- Provide a starting point for getting feedback so you can talk about how you're doing
- Celebrate successes and learn from failures

Most of us ignore this most of the time.

When we're doing big planning, we spend most of our time figuring out how the world around us will change if we just pull the right levers. We do number-crunching, analysis, four-box matrices, and detailing of who will do what. Conversations become an afterthought—something that gets bolted on to the "real" plan.

We call the bolted on stuff a Communication Plan. Because the two are not interwoven, conversations become public relations for the goals. This creates a Boom/Splat effect—great rollout and hype, quick fizzle, followed by lots of unanswered questions, confusion, and people doing their best to execute a plan they really don't understand.

When making little plans, our biggest mistake is lack of preparation for the conversation. "Oh…it's just a half-hour teleconference with teammates I've known for a long time. I'm sure I'm prepared." That shoot-from-the-hip attitude, combined with technology's ability to connect anybody to everybody, creates unbelievable amounts of complexity for those around us.

The Starter Kit for Simpler Work

Whether the plan is big or small, your role is to prepare for a successful conversation. This means that you organize everything in the plan so the discussion will make the most of everyone's time and attention. And it means that everyone should leave the discussion with enough clarity to manage themselves and the work of others.

This chapter focuses on getting you prepared for that kind of conversation. On the following pages are two easy-to-use tools based on the five building blocks for using people's time:

- **Know, Feel, Do**
- **Use to Succeed**

These tools can help simplify any project on any scale. They can be robust enough to help you organize your thinking on plans that took years to put together. Or they can be scaled down to help with 30 seconds of prep for that half-hour teleconference. Together, "Know, Feel, Do" and "Use to Succeed" are a starter kit for getting simple. When you use the tools you're saying, "We'll never have all the info we need. But here's the shortlist of what is necessary for clarity."

Doing the right planning also guarantees more and faster feedback. One of the main reasons feedback loops fall apart is because it takes too long for everyone to figure out what you really meant. In many companies, months after the rollout of some big plan, you will hear associates say, "Nowwww I get it. Why didn't they say that in the first meeting?" Get disciplined about what you bring to conversations and you'll find you get a lot more real-time feedback.

Final Prep: Things to Think About

There is a very specific reason why the five building blocks are linked together in separate tools:

- **Know, Feel, Do:** After you use this tool, clarity skyrockets.

Everyone knows enough to make informed choices. But do they know enough about how they are going to execute those choices, or how their success will be measured?

• **Use to Succeed:** That's where this tool comes in.

The two tools follow human nature. Many of us need intense discussion about our roles and behaviors (Know, Feel, Do) before we are ready to move on to how we will get things done (Use to Succeed).

These two tools have been designed to help you organize your thoughts. Frankly, it doesn't matter if no one but you or your immediate teammates see the tools. They are not for mass distribution. They are there to help you translate your thoughts, or those in The Plan, into a focused, meaningful conversation. One that changes how time gets used.

"In my experience, 95 percent of all the problems in organizations are due to conversations that didn't take place.

I don't know of anything that's more important than figuring out the different ways people need information and communicating accordingly."

DOUG FINTON, Human Dynamics International consultant

SIMPLE NOTES

- Many people with big titles shun the need for tools that organize their thinking…."That's why they pay me the big bucks." Hint: Use them in secret. Nobody needs to know how you got so clear so fast.
- Tailor the hell out of them! Don't get hung up on the wording or formatting provided here. What's critical is that you and your team get to do more thinking about the five building blocks: Know, Feel, Use, Do, and Succeed.
- With a little honesty, the tools will help you build self-awareness, promote learning, and contribute to your own continuous improvement. The tools will provide the most value:
  1. When you no longer need them. That is: Once the five building blocks are part of your everyday conversations.
  2. When you continue to use them anyway. That is: The completed tools are one-page project plans you can use for "managing up." Use the tools as discussion guides whenever you are contracting with someone who has budget or project approval.

Result: Instant clarity on where you are and are not aligned.

CHAPTER PUNCHLINE

Planning is about the design of conversation.
Because that's where people decide how time
and attention will get used.

"How we organize our thinking and information is really about how we understand what we're here to do.
Taxonomy, if done well, shows you the deep structure in everything."

JOSEPH COTHREL
Research Director
Arthur Andersen

"If there's one thing that changes the conversation and adds the most value, it's the ability to make sure your intent and purpose are really clear.
And not just In the head of the leader. But in the heart and behaviors too."

KATHLEEN BAKER
Hewlett-Packard Organization Design manager

GETTING STARTED
- Start small. After studying pages 66-69, go for a quick win.
- Keeping the five building blocks in mind, use the "Know, Feel, Do" tool to prep for a small effort (anything from a one-hour meeting to a two-month project). Or use the "Use to Succeed" tool to prep for a coaching opportunity.
- Don't try to get it perfect the first time. Most important is creating your own aha's. Figure out how the tools changed how you organized your thinking, questions, or information. Or how they got you to think about what the discussion would feel like for all those involved.
- After using either of the tools, ask your teammates or client for feedback on how conversations were different…and how the conversations changed buy-in, understanding, and implementation speed.
- After you've had a quick win, think about how both tools could change the next Big Plan.

Know, Feel, Do Tool

Goal: To make it easier to work smarter.
Helping people make informed, clear choices.

Sample Questions
(The right questions will lead you to the best tool. Tailor the tool for your role or project.)

Know: Right Data, Info, and Questions,
Right Way, Right Time

- Before talking to others: What data/info did I use to come to my conclusions on this issue?
- If I were limited to five minutes, what three things would I impart?
- Is my goal to teach them to fish or to feed them for a day? (Context and learning, or how-tos?)
- Am I delivering just-in-time learning?
- What questions will they have?
- What meaning or understanding must be common for everyone?
- etc.

Feel: Description of Buy-in, Commitment

- How will I know buy-in and commitment when I see it?
- How big of a change does buy-in/commitment to this project represent for people?
- What's my cutoff date for deciding if they are walking the talk?
- What do I want people to feel about their involvement and accountabilities?
- How will I know I was successful in creating that feeling?
- etc.

Do: Expectations, Behaviors

- What commitments and behaviors will people expect from me?
- What decisions do I want people to make? By when?
- What are the first steps in the process for me and my peers?
- What are the first steps in the process for everyone else?
- What are the triggers—changes that would shift my expectations?
- What will people do/say differently when we launch this project?
- etc.

Example

Sample completed tool from the perspective of a project leader launching a midsize project that is several months long. The details within the example are specific to this project. The project leader used this tool to organize a plan for her team, and to have a "managing up" discussion with the executive who sponsored the project.

Know, Feel, Do:
What "working smarter" will look like for this project

Our project team will:

Know **THE PROJECT PLAN**
- Understand the seven market forces behind this project and be able to articulate how the data changed the team's conclusions about what's important (need at least half a day of facilitated discovery to accomplish this goal)
- Understand our three key measures and be able to articulate their role in meeting those measures
- Understand and be able to articulate how this project connects to the company strategy

Feel **EXCITED YET ACCOUNTABLE**
- Excited about how [project's objectives] will put smiles on our customers' faces and make our associates' lives just a little bit less complicated by providing [project benefits]
- Accountable for removing the barriers to success (to be brainstormed during half-day discovery session)

Do **WHAT IT TAKES**
- Manage the "noise"—objections about the difficulties of this project—by doing [work to be brainstormed]
- Team members regularly communicate and reinforce their role, the three key measures, and how this project connects to The Plan
- Assume shared accountability for the team's/project's success

Use to Succeed Tool

Goal: To spend less time working harder, making it easier to succeed

Sample Questions

(The right questions lead you to the best tool. Tailor the tool for your role or project.)

Success: Clear enough so teammates can manage themselves

- What are my project definitions for success on Results, Milestones, Behaviors?
- How are those definitions aligned with The Plan?
- Does the person to whom I report define success in the same way?
- How are my teammates currently defining success?
- What's the difference between my definition and theirs?
- How new is this conversation? (What can I assume has been discussed before?)
- etc.

Use: Right Tools, Training, and Support, Right Way, Right Time

- If I'm not involved in day-to-day project activities, who can answer questions or facilitate the team's work by answering all of the following questions?
- How much learning curve/development time must be allowed?
- Tools, support, resources, processes, technology: What already exists that can be used?
- What will have to be created?
- How many people resources are needed? And what skills must they possess?
- How many people resources are coming from "inside"? How many from "outside"?
- How will we prevent "Boom/Cplat"? What ongoing support will be needed after rollout?
- etc.

Example

Sample completed tool from the perspective of a project leader launching a midsize project that is several months long. The details within the example are specific to this project. The project leader used this tool to organize a plan for her team, and to have a "managing up" discussion with the executive who sponsored the project.

Use to Succeed:
What success will look like and how we will get there

For this project:

Success **IS SPEED, VALUE, AND OPPORTUNITY FOR GROWTH**
- Speed: Cut the time associates spend on this activity in half
- Value: Which should drive customer satisfaction up 12–13 points
- Growth: Expect to free 10,000 associate hours to be used on market-killer Project X

Use **BRAINPOWER AND OUR INTRANET...FOR NOW**
- Due to short turnaround time and low budget, we've specifically selected a team that has worked together before and needs no additional training or tools.
- But once we move into pilot implementation, we'll need to deliver a suite of tools and training including [team to brainstorm ideas]. Currently, we have no budget for these tools. Monies must be allocated after brainstorming.
- Team will brainstorm about data sources and people sources needed to assist development.

THE TOOLS ORGANIZE WHAT THE BRAIN NEEDS

"Here are some fundamentals of how individuals change their behaviors:

1. Adults need to be really clear on the *reasons* for taking on new information or doing things differently. Up until the age of 13 or so, your brain is designed to make any and all connections needed to change. But by the time you reach 20, your brain is happy to keep doing what it has already learned to do. You must work to change it. That's where reasons come in.

2. The science of information processing says it's useful to hook new stuff to something you already know.

3. Emotions will not be denied. Once an emotion is created, it lives as chemicals in your system. If it's a strong emotion, your body is flooded with an array of chemicals coursing through your system at the cellular level. In other words, you can't think rationally if you've got emotional blocks. Clarity also gets blocked. Nothing goes to the higher cognitive structures in the cerebrum until it passes through the amygdala—the 'seat of emotions.' Said simply, you have to use emotions to create the right kind of thinking."

"The big challenge in this century will be for people to consciously understand, and acknowledge their emotional intelligence just like cognitive intelligence—and bring those two things into harmony."

DR. MICHAEL O'BRIEN, psychologist

Chapter 6

Contracting

Behavioral communication

This is the very coinage of your brain.

William Shakespeare, *Hamlet*

"It's a much more respectful way of communicating with people. You're treating them as thinking adults." Julie Thompson, VP of HR and Training for California Pizza Kitchens, is referring to what happens when you bring Know, Feel, Use, Do, and Succeed into daily conversations.

Many conversations begin with the goal of sharing information. This is a waste of time. Today there are more efficient ways to get that info. The goal of most conversations should be to clarify, question, reflect, and engage. Somewhere in the middle of all that—and for many of us, unknowingly—the dialogue turns into contracting—who will do what, by when, etc. The act of contracting demands a lot more discipline and clarity.

The last two chapters focused on getting ready for that moment. Even if it was just 30 seconds of prep for a call or an email, the previous tools helped you get clear before using anyone else's time and attention. Now what?

Behavioral Communication Model

During our study, we looked at how people *really* make decisions—what information they need to take action. A pattern emerged. Everyone, everywhere—from the most junior person to the most senior—had just five questions. (See the Behavioral Communication Model on the next page.) If you focus on getting these questions answered, conversations quickly and easily transform into action. Buy-in and understanding just

BEHAVIORAL COMMUNICATION MODEL

• How is this relevant to what I do?

• What, specifically, should I do?

• How will I be measured, and what are the consequences?

• What tools and support are available?

• WIIFM—What's in it for me? For us?

QUIZ

WHICH OF THE FIVE QUESTIONS IS ASKED MOST?

BACKGROUND: Let's say you hold a town meeting and 100 people attend. You do your best to explain some change, like the new strategic plan. During the Q&A session, everyone asks for more information.

GUARANTEE: 60 percent of the questions will *always* be one of the five listed in the Behavioral Communication Model above.

QUESTION: Which one is it?

ANSWER: The most asked question relates to execution—the tool and support question. You probably thought it was "WIIFM?" didn't you? Most people fail this quiz. Go back and reread Chapters 2, 3, and 4. Between two-thirds and three-quarters of us are missing the skills or tools we need to successfully do everything that comes at us. Yet most communication spends the *least* time on tools and support. And we wonder why we have so much work complexity!

Qualifier: All people are different. All changes are different. The 60 Percent Rule of Tools and Support is a guideline for the total population. As you will see elsewhere in this chapter, change agents and executives rarely believe tools and support is a top need.

happen. And you can begin to change how time gets used.

The anatomy of a decision to act involves the following five questions.

How is this relevant to what I do? Think of this as Marketing 101. If you can't make your ideas relevant to the individuals in front of you within the first five minutes or the first page, assume you've lost them. Everyone has too much to focus on. If we paid full attention to everything that is *supposed* to be relevant, we'd never get anything done. Your topic is relevant if you can connect it to how people currently spend their time and attention. For example: If you want to talk about The New Strategy, begin the conversation with your team's current priorities. Then describe how The New Strategy is different. Or if you need a busy executive to sign on as your team's sponsor, describe how your charter relates to her top three priorities. Fail to make these kinds of connections quickly and you'll fail to get people's full attention.

What, specifically, should I do? Again, this is not a call for returning to command and control. Instead, your expectations must be crystal clear. What are the immediate next steps? What are all the steps in the process? Who has accountability for each? How will people know if those accountabilities shift? You need to communicate the answers—up front.

How will I be measured and what are the consequences? Although it's helpful if the answer is part of your performance management process, you needn't be anal about "measurement." This doesn't have to lead to analysis paralysis. People just need to hear—up front—how they will know they're doin' good. What will success look like? How often will they get feedback? Sometimes it can be a from-your-gut discussion. But it must be discussed.

People also need to understand the consequences of success or failure. A consequence can be positive or negative. It can mean "Here's how the customer will benefit as a direct result of our efforts." It can also mean, "Jane, down in Shipping, won't be able to do her job if we miss this deadline."

What tools and support are available? This question is all about execution—getting everything done. Again, most people don't have the tools to do their job. Or when they do, most tools are underused or misunderstood. Anything you can do to help people make the connection between what they have to do and the available tools can be extremely powerful. Here's a partial listing of tools for knowledge work:

- Training
- IT (Notes, the Net, etc.)
- Coaching
- Additional budget
- Communication kit
- Meetings, offsites
- Communities of practice
- Mentoring
- Additional time
- Sponsorship or champions
- Info organized for the specific task
- Additional people
- Dedicated space/place
- Research data

Your role in making that connection is huge. Right tools, right time, right way shorten everyone's 'to do' list and helps them focus. If you don't use the right tools, at the right time, in the right way—with training to use them properly—lots of time and attention get wasted.

WIIFM—What's in it for me? For us? Although it's helpful if the answer to this question involves a formal reward and recognition process, it doesn't have to. The answer can be a lot less "costly." Like: less stress, more fun, enhanced teamwork, more time with one's family.

Also keep in mind the rule mentioned in the quiz on page 72. This is not the most asked question. While all five questions should be addressed, Tools and Support is often the biggest gap.

The Model in Action

Julie Thompson of California Pizza Kitchens knows firsthand how the model works. "I was trying to get Operations to make one of our training programs mandatory. I explained that there were serious legal ramifications if our store directors didn't get and act on this training. No matter how hard I tried, I kept getting, 'We have more important things to do like run our restaurants and serve our guests than getting the directors to sit through your class.' I kept wondering 'Why aren't they getting this?'"

"Then I remembered the five questions," Thompson continued. "The next meeting I spent just a few minutes explaining how this training program was relevant to sales and guest satisfaction. How we'd measure the results. How the training was a time-efficient tool for directors… etc. Suddenly, they saw the light. Approved!"

"I had the same results in the field. I went from needing nine months to get everyone signed up to pulling it off in just weeks. I did it

THEORY CORNER

WHY THE BEHAVIORAL COMMUNICATION MODEL WORKS

Most important: Because it "forces" empathy. It helps you examine what you want to communicate from the listener's point of view—not yours or the company's. Second, think of it as a balanced scorecard for making and acting on a decision. It touches everything we draw upon to do knowledge work:

- Intellectual needs
- Social and emotional needs
- Infrastructure and support
- Focus and expectations
- Measurement systems
- Rewards and recognition systems

It combines the cognitive theories of Jean Piaget, Jerome Bruner, and others with what psychologist Frederick Herzberg called hygiene factors—the things we need in place to get stuff done.

Finally, the model works because human nature abhors a vacuum. If you don't provide answers to these five questions, the grapevine or rumor mill will. Often, incorrectly.

CHAPTER PUNCHLINE

Behavioral communication gets people what they need to act. Quickly.

Which jump-starts working smarter.

through cover memos in which I wrote about a paragraph to answer each of the five questions."

Kim Thomas is a communication director for Ameritech. She connects the five questions to such successes as helping call centers double the number of leads fed to the sales force and making an IT conversion "virtually flawless with total buy-in and support from everyone." But for her, the model's biggest value is as a strategic thinking tool.

"It's proven to be an effective gap-analysis tool. While we're still in the planning stage, we uncover deficiencies that would have hindered success. Most typically, we've found we need to establish clearer

USING BEHAVIORAL COMMUNICATION EVERY DAY

	MOST EFFICIENT	MOST PRAGMATIC	IDEAL
FORMAT	**EMAILS, VOICEMAILS, RECAPPING NEXT STEPS** Answer recipient's five questions within your message. (One page or less)	**MEETINGS, FACE-TO-FACE CONVERSATIONS** Provide a couple of the answers as "givens." Get confirmation. Brainstorm the remaining answers as a team.	**OFFSITES, COACHING, TRAINING** Facilitate discussion about a larger strategy. Have the individual discover the five answers on his/her own.
UPSIDE	Speed, efficiency, and clarity	Alignment, clarity, and making the best use of everyone's time	Complete ownership of the answers
DOWNSIDE	Poor choice of media if: • You're contracting for a major shift in behaviors. • You haven't established a relationship or rapport with the recipient. • There is no common context (like a strategy).	If you have a good team leader, there should be minimal or no downside.	Time-intensive and requires exceptional coaching/facilitation skills.

measures and develop a broader arsenal of tools and support to equip people to make the change." Her point is important. Figuring out which answers you *don't* have helps you to be proactive in designing change. Making the complex clear is a change management tool.

It can also be a leadership tool. CITGO CEO Dave Tippeconnic recently took his senior team through a major change process. "At our offsite, we had everyone answer the five questions to explain how they would take their new assignments into the organization. I just got back from a site visit, and I can see how the clarity had an impact on implementing our strategies."

Tippeconnic continued, "When you focus on what's next for people, what they need to do and what tools they can use, you really move the process forward. You take away the arguments that come up due to lack of clarity. That is a big benefit."

SIMPLE NOTES

Three-Minute Guarantee: If you've used the tools in Chapter 5— "Know, Feel, Do" and "Use to Succeed"—to organize your thinking, you'll need only a couple minutes of prep for any contracting conversation.

Human Nature Guarantee: We're all very busy. Common sense says most of your teammates will jump into answering *other people's* five questions without organizing their own thinking. If you're the exception to that rule, you'll always be the team leader known for using time and attention effectively.

Grand Poobah Guarantee: There is a running joke about CEOs: "If it has a staple in it, it doesn't get read." Unfortunately, for some senior execs, the joke is reality. The higher up you go, the more you've got to be able to answer the five questions in one page or less.

GETTING STARTED

- Just do it! Try the model within 48 hours of reading this chapter. Don't worry about perfecting the answers, just cover them—in an email, a meeting, or a telephone call. Your quick win will give you the encouragement you need to use the model again and again.
- If you used the tools in Chapter 5, you probably found and addressed some gaps there. Answering the five questions gives you another opportunity to develop clearer measures, a broader arsenal of tools and support, etc., before you launch a change.

SHARED MINDSET QUIZ

We all know how Mission/Vision/Values and Strategies are *supposed* to work. They are the frameworks you expect others to use to answer their own questions. If you believe frameworks currently serve you well, take the following test:

1. Randomly select 100 people
2. *Don't* ask them about the company's Prime Directive.
   Do ask them the five behavioral questions.
3. Prepare to be horrified when you hear the results. Many companies find that the mindset and road maps they present are not translating into a shared view of how real work gets done or what's needed to get it done.

MOST OF US

**LIFE FOLLOWS A
BELL CURVE**

WHAT BEHAVIORAL COMMUNICATION TEACHES YOU

EARLY ADOPTERS

When it is necessary to change behaviors, early adopters answer the five questions intuitively—in nanoseconds. Most will get bored or impatient with any attempt to confirm how they answered the questions.
(This can be a problem when the early-changer is a senior exec. He/she has changed but often can't clearly articulate why and how. The result may be a leadership problem down the road.)

THE MODEL WORKS IN THE "REAL" WORLD TOO

Josh was five years old when he was diagnosed with epilepsy. By six, he experienced seizures known as "drop attacks." Up to 20 times a day he would completely lose all muscle control. His parents, Sue and Dave, reached out to Teresa Schaefer. Schaefer organizes community resource teams for children in need. When asked what she did to get multiple teams all working seamlessly to meet Josh's needs, she said her job was to organize meetings around the behavioral communication model.

For example:

- Teachers, the school nurse, and physicians all had defined accountabilities. (What should I do?)
- Strategies were put in place to shorten response times to Josh's seizures. (Measures and consequences)
- And when Josh went to school sporting a helmet and kneepads (tools designed to protect him), his classmates sponsored "helmet day." They all wore helmets as a show of support and team unity. (Their view of: What's in it for us?)

MOST OF US

This model is of most help to the 60 to 70 percent of us who fall in the middle of the bell curve. Clarity is all we needed to be more creative, focused, flexible, and responsive.

THOSE RESISTING CHANGE

Use the model to take them out. You don't have the time to waste on them!

If you've followed the behavioral model in multiple conversations (so you're absolutely certain the issue isn't your lack of clarity), and they still haven't changed, they never will—no matter how often you get clear on the five questions.

Chapter 7

Listening and Scanning

Hit delete, find the good stuff

When people talk, listen completely. Most people never listen.

Ernest Hemingway, whose lifelong goal was to write one true sentence

Here is how it's supposed to work: Use shared mindset, team goals, or The Strategy to filter everything coming at you.

Let's test that. Today you got 128 emails, 47 voicemails, had countless conversations and interruptions while trying to skim all that "must read" material, and you attended 4 meetings. How often did you use The Strategy to figure out what to delete, what to answer and which meeting was important?

That's what I thought. The bad news: Because most of us don't know what to scan for, we make too many poor choices. One of the emails you just deleted had a lot to do with The Strategy. Only you missed it because the communication was unclear. Or you focused on the seven things from your boss or customer and blew off everything else. Short term, that may seem efficient. Long term, where does that leave your personal growth and control over your own workflow?

The good news: You are now well versed in the five basics. Know, Feel, Use, Do, and Succeed are the foundation for organizing everyday work. Applied to planning (Chapter 5), they help you organize your thinking. Turn them into questions (Chapter 6), and they help you communicate. You can also use the same five building blocks to focus your listening and scanning.

The Goal of Day-to-Day Listening

We listen in many different ways. There's empathy, what you would use when listening to a friend who is going through a tough time. There's listening for coaching, to help someone see things about himself. There's listening to discover new ways of thinking. The list is endless.

But most of us spend most of our time doing day-to-day listening. We try to make sense of everything coming at us. Figuring out where to spend our time.

Because your time is the most valuable asset you have, improving day-to-day listening can deliver huge returns. It frees up just a few more seconds, minutes, or hours and makes them available for doing something else. The focus of this chapter is compressing the list of what should get your attention, so you can spend time on what is important.

The more surgical you can be when you listen, the more you'll find the good stuff.

The goal is simple: Have a specific, concise listening strategy. Or get buried.

Knowing What to Listen For

On the next page is the same five-question model we saw in Chapter 6. This time it is organized and rephrased slightly for listening. Just remember CLEAR. To find clarity among the noise, every conversation, meeting, and email should be scanned with the following items in mind:

• **CONNECTED TO WHAT I DO.** Far too many people are calling you into meetings and asking you to read stuff without being clear about how these things connect to your top priorities. They are asking you to take the time to figure it out, when they didn't. If it's an email or voicemail, and you can't figure out what connection it has to your top priorities within 15 seconds, hit delete. The person who wrote the communication does not respect your time. Anyone who does will at least attempt to make the connection clear. If it's a meeting and the team leader isn't clear, ask, "Help me understand how this is connected to what I do." After several minutes of dialogue, if you still don't see a connection, that person was not prepared to use your time. Be polite, but excuse yourself. Staying in that meeting is a waste of your time.

• **LIST OF NEXT STEPS.** If the communication is electronic and there is no "call to action" or next steps, same thing…hit delete. The sender is

FINDING CLARITY AMIDST THE NOISE

C	**CONNECTED TO WHAT I DO**	(How is this relevant?)
L	**LIST OF NEXT STEPS**	(What should I do?)
E	**EXPECTATIONS**	(What does success look like?)
A	**ABILITY**	(What tools and support do I need?)
R	**RETURN**	(WIIFM: What's in it for me? For us?)

A LEADER'S VIEW OF HITTING DELETE, FINDING THE GOOD STUFF

"The challenge for me is sorting through the layers of complexity and deciding what to focus on. Input management has become a huge challenge. I could do nothing all day but read, respond, read, respond. I would feel like a telecommunications switch. So I don't. Many of the requests will never hear from me. I'd rather spend time with my team. My best time management is hitting delete then spending time with my team creating common understanding and meaning. Or just getting to know them as people. Around here, we call that the background of relatedness. It's really about deepening relationships. In the long run, that gives you better business results."

JOHN LECHLEITER, SVP, Pharmaceutical Products, Eli Lilly

someone who thinks he's adding value by creating dots for you to filter. If the meetings you attend don't end with a recap of who will do what in the next few days (not months!), get assigned to a different team. The project leader is not focused on action or clarifying accountabilities. This is just wasting your time.

- **EXPECTATIONS.** With so much change, it's rare for anyone to know what success looks like in a first discussion. But if you've been in several meetings or exchanged several emails with no progress toward a definition of success and how that affects what is expected of you, hit delete. Apply to be assigned to a different team. Do what it takes to distance yourself from this team or leader. The team may get where it's going, but only after wasting a lot of your time. (Or, better yet, take the lead in bringing clarity to project expectations. You'll be noticed as the team member who competed on clarity.)

    Remember the three criteria for success mentioned in Chapter 4: Business results, project milestones, and behavior (how you should be spending your time and attention). Different people need different levels of detail on each. Do not leave those meetings until you're satisfied you have enough details about success to manage yourself.

- **ABILITY.** In a recent article, "Managing Oneself," Peter Drucker stated, "Amazingly few people know how they get things done." Your job is to know how you get stuff done   which tools and support increase your ability to tackle the list. Be a proactive listener. Ask lots of "ability" questions: Who are the right people to pull this off? How do we get the right data and information? Is it organized to meet our needs? Do we need to call in a content expert?…etc. (For more help, reread anything relating to tools and support in the last three chapters.)

    Also, it's important to be realistic. Assume you will get some assignments for which neither the answers nor the tools are sufficient. That's just life. But if you are seeing a pattern of too few tools, too little training, on too many teams, too often—call a headhunter. Your time is being wasted.

- **RETURN.** Ditto on what's in this for you. Be realistic—there are lots of projects we do because we have to. But if you're seeing a pattern in which too many projects offer too little personal return, hit delete.

(WIIFM doesn't have to be compensation. It can be less stress, more focus, more fun, etc.)

Your Accountabilities as a Listener

All that deleting frees up lots of time! But you have to earn the right to hit delete that often. Among your accountabilities:

---

1. USE COMMON SENSE. Of course, the email from your brother deserves time and attention. Even if he's never been CLEAR in his entire life.

---

2. KNOW THYSELF. Know which one of the five questions is most important to you. For many CEOs, it's relevance. Many leaders are essentially responsible for everything, and they get far too many requests for their attention. They have to be ever-vigilant about "pushing down" anything that is not relevant to their chosen top few priorities.

For a change agent, the priority might be expectations. You probably feel comfortable discovering everything else as the project evolves. But if you can't get an executive or sponsor to define what success looks like and how that definition influences what is expected of you, you're setting yourself up for failure. Most change agents have learned the hard way to walk away from such situations.

For a new trainee, the priority might be getting absolute clarity on what tools and support he needs to use. You will want to take the time to figure out which of the five questions is most important to you most often. Whichever is most important, be proactive. Get what you need to make informed decisions.

---

3. PRE-DELETE, BE A COACH. Just because you know how to be CLEAR, doesn't mean everyone else does. Before you delete other people's efforts, do a few minutes of coaching. Hand them the five-question behavioral communication model. Show them CLEAR. Tell them that, as a listener, this is what you'll be looking for. Most people want to do the right thing.

---

4. SEE PATTERNS. Looking at how you listen, and how to improve, is one of your most important self awareness tools. Even after just a few meetings or emails, the CLEAR model can help you see how you listen. As you look at the table on page 85, the goal is to be in the

LISTENING PATTERNS

	VICTIM	PRAGMATIST	PRO-ACTIVIST
SPENDS THE MOST TIME	**LISTENING FOR LIST OF NEXT STEPS**	**ANSWERING TOO MANY** emails/voicemails and attending too many meetings. Has no concise listening strategy.	**FREEING TIME** Has a concise listening strategy. Is surgical in determining what gets deleted.
LISTENING PATTERN	To change behaviors, needs to be fed the five answers. Rarely, if ever, says "Help me understand…"	Gets day-to day stuff done, but misses new opportunities. Knows which of the five questions the boss or company cares about. Gets clear on those. Too busy to get clarity on all five.	After deleting the "noise," usually needs clarification on just one or two of the questions. Still asks about all five building blocks to be clear when communicating with others.
STRATEGY TO IMPROVE	Change—fast. Behind your back, everyone says you're resisting change. First focus: Get clear on tools and support.	Pick one or two of the five that are not being answered. Continuously ask about them. You are prepping to be a better communicator.	Continuous self-assessment and improvement. (If not necessary, apply for Supreme Being status.)

"Right now, in Corporate America, there isn't the critical mass of people who know how to listen. **The companies that will survive and prosper** are the ones that see it now and start creating that capability."

CATHY CARMODY, freelance Organizational Electrician
(Change agent in corporate energy and connections)

right-hand column as often as possible. Do a self-evaluation: What percentage of your time is spent in each of the three columns?

Finding the Good Stuff

An amazing thing happens when you have a precise listening strategy. Theorists call it "order for free." The good stuff suddenly appears. Out of nowhere. In reality, most of it was there all along. It was just so damned hard to see it in the tsunami's swirl of choices and data. Be more surgical in how you listen and scan, and the good stuff will find you.

SIMPLE NOTES

"But my manager is the one wasting my time. I can't hit delete on her meetings!" If this is your situation, what you do will always come down to two things:

1. **Use common sense.** Choose carefully when and how to hit delete.
2. **It's your choice to waste your own time.**
   She can't waste your time without your consent. God gave you 1,440 minutes today. You assign those minutes to your manager. Choose carefully who you let use your minutes.

GETTING STARTED

Just do it!

CHAPTER PUNCHLINE

Knowing what to listen for frees up time

"When I first came into this job, I eliminated

two-thirds of the paper I got. There are maybe four to five things you can track. What's important is figuring out what they are, how you do them, and how you make them useful in running the business. That frees you to have an inquisitive mind—to be restlessly discontent with the status quo."

MEL GOODES, retired CEO, Warner-Lambert

"Listening in this way [CLEAR] holds pretty close

to truth. The first thing I want to sniff out is 'Am I the right person to take the action?' As I go through the questions, I'm trying to figure out what's important. Is this a creative idea that is well-defined and, if done right, drives huge productivity gains? Or is this something we'll spend a lot of time on and the payback is unclear? We don't have the time for those."

DAVE JOHNSON, head of Manufacturing for 20 General Mills plants

"Email is the great leveler. Everybody copies you on everything. Every day I have to be very focused in what I look at and what I spend time on. I fight to keep my calendar focused on things that really count."
MATT KISSNER, CEO, Pitney Bowes Financial Services

Chapter 8

Engaging

Bringing it all together for the right kind of order

Drama is life with the dull bits cut out.

Alfred Hitchcock, master storyteller

By now, you've probably seen a pattern throughout this section. Changing how time gets used is really about disciplined thinking and sharing. For you and for your teammates, simplicity and working smarter mean organizing your thoughts and creating clarity before jumping in.

But what if you need to create clarity beyond your team? For hundreds or thousands of people? The day-to-day basics discussed in the previous chapters—which tools to use, the expectations, the specific next steps, and all the rest—might be helpful to have in the background, but it would be too detailed to be useful for that many people. You would need to look for something that easily creates common meaning and purpose for everyone. That something is storytelling.

"When the story is in your mind…you see its relevance to something happening in your own life," said famed mythologist Joseph Campbell. "It gives you perspective on what's happening to you. There is such a feeling…of a deep, rich, life-vivifying sort that you don't want to give it up." [1]

Stories captivate us. Engage us. Social historians believe stories are the glue that binds together societies, cultures, families, and religion. Such is the power of storytelling.

Because they cut through the noise, quickly making the complex clear, stories can be an important business tool. This chapter is about using storytelling as a business tool to engage hundreds or even thousands of people.

Storytelling Restructures the Basics

With a nod to Hitchcock, corporate storytelling is Know, Feel, Use, Do and Succeed with all the dull bits cut out. This changes how you use the content of the five basics—they morph into a more captivating framework. The structure of the story becomes more important than the details for each of the five building blocks.

Throughout time, and in all cultures around the world, storytelling has followed a universal structure. Cavewomen grunting about their mates' couch potato habits, Hollywood's latest effort, and everything in between—all adhere to a basic framework:

1. Conflict
2. Transition
3. Climax
4. Close

This construct organizes life into drama. It draws us in as active listeners.

More important than being able to spin a strategic yarn is understanding the power of this four-part structure—and how you will waste time and attention if you ignore it.

For example, most strategic plans are organized according to some economic or marketplace logic. Like, "This is what's happening in Hong Kong, and since our competitor produces more goods over there, we need to do blahblahblah in order to succeed." That may be valid competitive logic. But most people don't *listen* that way. The four parts of storytelling can help you organize your thoughts and strategies to fit how people listen.

A Story About the Order of Ideas

"For the last 20 years, I've basically been a change agent. Fourteen of those years at Duracell," says plant manager John Parks. "Each time I've changed jobs, it has been to implement massive change." Parks felt secure in that role, facing tough situations and never feeling intimidated. Until one moment in 1998, at a new job in Lancaster, South Carolina.

"Before I started, there were some meetings to introduce me as the next plant manager. Let me tell you, it was hostile. Morale was lousy. I'm sitting there thinking, 'Oh my God, what am I walking into?' It wasn't Duracell's fault. It was just that so much had changed in this

MESSAGE MAP™
STORYTELLING AS BUSINESS TOOL

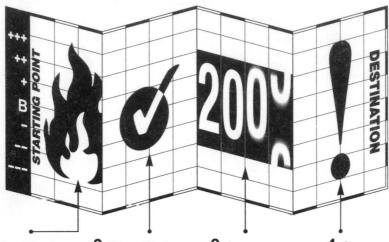

1 **Our "Burning Platform"** *
- The only choice is to change
- The business case

2 **Where We Are**
- Progress to date
- Celebrate accomplishments, recognize shortcomings
- Communicate progress

3 **Success This Year**
- Current year business objectives/priorities
- Usual format: Balanced scorecard

4 **Our Destination**
- Mission (can also include Vision, Values, and Principles)

---

* Commonly used phrase coined by Daryl Conner, head of ODR consulting. Based on a real-life oil rig explosion and the need to make very tough choices

THE COMPLETED TOOL

A completed one-page story is a mix of headlines (for sound-bite clarity and emotional pull) and bullet points about measures and work to be done. The Message Map is then used to guide conversations about corporate change and strategies. Think of it as a one-page guide for *any* Big Picture discussion. You can download this and other one-page examples from *Simplicity's* companion website: http://www.simplerwork.com

plant so fast—there were too many fixes on top of fixes on top of fixes. The senior team I report to wanted me to address both profitability and people problems—fast. So I knew I had to listen carefully and respond clearly."

"To do that I needed to start with a very focused story about the past few years and how the next 12 months would be different. That's where the Message Map came in." Parks is referring to one way to use the four-part anatomy of storytelling—organizing change and strategic plans as stories (see page 90).

Parks quickly assembled his team. They did lots of listening to people in the plant, and then, for a full day, they brain-dumped. Everything they knew about the history and the future of the plant was organized according to the storytelling structure, translated for business purposes.

STORYTELLING STRUCTURE	BUSINESS TRANSLATION
Conflict	**Burning Platform**
Transition	**Where We Are** (Successes or progress to date)
Climax	**Success This Year**
Close	**Destination** (Mission, can also include Vision, Values)

"There were two reasons it was so easy for me to use a tool based on storytelling," says Parks. "First, it made sense. It took all the thoughts that we'd get to eventually and just organized them. It was so easy to understand. Second, it was simple to use. No fancy equations about the psyche of people. It just said, 'Put yourself in the seat of the person in the audience and listen.' It took the complexities out of our situation and made sense of them. I had all the information. The tool just organized it in the way people needed to hear it."

Parks didn't get any time to rehearse his story. As soon as it was ready, he convened the first all-hands meeting since he had arrived at the plant. The meeting room could accommodate just over 75 people. He had to meet with over 1,000 employees from four different shifts. So 13 one-hour meetings were scheduled over 36 hours. About 20 minutes of each meeting was reserved for questions.

Conflict. Parks began his story by making the competitive case for change. Duracell had just lost Sam's Warehouse Club to a competitor,

(Energizer), because its cost structure was out of whack. (That loss directly affected this plant's production numbers.) Everything in this part of the story was data driven. People needed the facts behind management's plan for change.

Parks also showed empathy and connected with all 1,000 employees by talking about what *any* audience cares about most— their view of the situation. In making the case for change, he also included what he'd learned about plant morale. He quoted one of the remarks heard during his first visit to the plant—"We're treated like dogs around here"— and showed everyone the employee survey data that echoed the sentiment.

Transition. Next he cited the successes that everyone at the plant had achieved over the past few months. They ranged from the smallest things, like having the restrooms painted, to breakthroughs like how everyone in the plant was asked for ideas and solutions. Parks needed to show that he and his team were walking the talk during the transition. Again, this part of the story was data driven. Not even Parks' team had realized how much was already in the works until they were pushed to itemize everything to tell the story.

Climax. Parks spent the most time organizing his thoughts in the part of the story where everything would either fall apart or come together—how he defined success for that year. To get costs under control, he would have to completely change the shift rotation. The current configuration was just costing too much money.

People's lives would be altered. Some personal income—in the form of overtime—would go away. And when a plant employs over a thousand people in a town like Lancaster, South Carolina, with a population of 10,000, the impact of this change could go beyond Duracell. It could affect the community.

Parks believed in the power of storytelling. And his faith was about to be tested. After doing his best to provide people what they needed to make informed decisions, Parks opened the floor for questions.

In 12 of the 13 meetings, the very first questions were always the same: "How do we get Sam's Club back?" Business focused. Not me-focused.

Sure, there were some naysayers. But on the whole, Parks' beliefs were confirmed. Most people wanted to make a difference. They just

THEORY CORNER

STORIES GO TO SCHOOL

Dr. Janet Greco is an instructor in the Organizational
Development Masters Program at the University of
Pennsylvania. She says her work "uses concepts from
action learning, collaborative inquiry, and story inquiry to
help executives study their own assumptions." According
to Greco, "On the whole, as social animals we're not very
skilled at understanding what moves us and others.
Stories help us. They address the kind of learning
that our world demands of managers: Saying more with less;
finding ways to live with ambiguity; looking for alternatives to
mechanistic rationality as the only arbiter of response.
I know from experience that stories are powerful teaching
tools. The discipline of narrative has something to offer
our organizations. It not only provides an organizing
framework for analysis, probability, and proofs; it adds the
motivational power of symbols, truth, coherency, and fidelity."

"Storytelling is how human beings

relate to each other. Not through business plans.
The more senior you are, the more you learn through
storytelling."

JIM CHAMPY, author, *Reengineering Management* and *The Arc of Ambition*

needed to understand the complexities of the situation, and they needed a leader who could provide focus and clarity on the necessary changes.

Close. At the end of his presentation, Parks discussed the new mission of the plant. Since its rollout, the mission—"Flexible, Focused, and Responsive"—has helped to unify a thousand people. But Parks knew that the mission should not get the most emphasis during his first meetings with everyone in the plant. At that moment, it would be heard as too much fluff, too little proof of action.

The first phase of the shift change started immediately. At the end of each meeting, Parks announced that a design team would be formed to guide the shift change. He asked for volunteers—needing about 15 line workers for the team. Four hundred volunteered that day. All this at a plant where, just weeks earlier, Parks had wondered what he'd gotten himself into.

The ripple effects of those meetings continue to be felt today. Parks reports that in his first year, plant performance improved between 30 and 40 percent in six key areas. "But just as important to me," says Parks with a smile, "is walking down an aisle in the plant and having people wave. I can't even see their face they're so far away. But they wave. That was not the case a year ago!"

Clearly, these results would not be possible without a leader like John Parks. So where does storytelling fit in this leader's toolkit? "The beauty of the structure is how it formats and focuses everything in your head. It allows you to get your thoughts in the right flow, makes you think it through. And if you go in with strong leadership, it's a home run."

When a Story Is More Than a Story

If you have skimmed through this book, you've probably discovered that Section 3 is about changing the infrastructure to make things simpler. That idea actually starts here, in storytelling. The companies that make real progress use stories to change more than the hearts and minds of people.

They ask, "Have we changed our feedback systems to ensure that we can accurately report successes to date?" and "How has our story changed how teams are working together?" If your story follows the four-part structure, it should change how work gets done.

For example: Bank of America has been using Message Maps for years. "I know this was originally developed as a communication tool," says Kathy McLeod, of the bank's leadership development team, "But we continue to use it to help leaders organize their thinking. When a senior team is asked to put its entire strategic plan on just one page, the discussion gets very involved. Everyone gets engaged!"

Jim Shanley, who heads that team, focuses on leveraging the moment of engagement. "We've used this tool on dozens of important initiatives," says Shanley. "But the most successful were when we used shared mindset at the senior level to drive big changes throughout the organization. The 'Freedom to Act' initiative is an example."

"We were trying to give all associates in our consumer bank the freedom to act smarter and to eliminate any dumb things we might be doing. The Message Map and shared mindset gave us a starting point. To truly deliver freedom to act, we had to follow up on everything that was set in motion. Selection and performance systems were changed. A follow-up tool, 'Roadmap to Success,' was created to further guide implementation efforts. New feedback systems were built." Shanley reinforces, "All were tied back to the original 'Freedom to Act' Message Map."

CITGO CEO Dave Tippeconnic has also experienced the power of linking everything back to the map. Huge mergers and recent changes in oil prices have created havoc throughout his industry. "But when you look at our competitive position," says Tippeconnic, "what really distinguishes any company from another is how effectively you use the talents of your people. It's just obvious that you are not going to capture that value if you can't communicate effectively and have everyone leading from the same page."

Recently, 60 CITGO executives came together to develop their Message Map. Tippeconnic needed to ensure complete alignment on the company's strategies and expose whatever issues could pull the team in different directions.

After a brief training session, teams were organized and separated by business unit. They were told that they had until 8 A.M. the next morning to create their own strategic story. Every team would tell its story in a one-page Message Map. Tippeconnic and his direct reports had the same assignment.

Into the evening, they all referred to spreadsheets and financial

THEORY CORNER

HOW THE ANATOMY OF A STORY HELPS US LEARN

"Any process that follows conflict, transition, climax, and close is identical to the four conditions needed for learners to experience conceptual change. If they're going to bridge a gap in their own thinking, they need to

- Experience dissatisfaction with the current way
- Be able to understand the 'new way'
- Be able to see the new way as plausible and useful
- Be able to use the new way to continuously adapt to change"

DR. SUSAN LAND, Assistant Professor, Instructional Systems, Penn State

"We've more than doubled in size in the last year. We've found we have to spend a lot of time creating **the right story...**the right metaphor. The goal is for every person to have something to measure against when they do something as simple as pick up the phone."

CLEMENT MOK, Chief Creative Officer, Sapient

CHAPTER PUNCHLINE

Your story is the list of what's important.

And it should fit on one page.

plans, then they turned the data into stories. For some, this was difficult. Translating numbers and projections into stories is not usually required of managers. But by the morning, every team had a story to tell. To make sure that his views didn't hinder the exchange of ideas, Tippeconnic and his team would present last, not first.

By the third presentation, patterns had begun to emerge. The teams began to see a lot of alignment where they thought there was none. All the definitions of success—where numbers and targets were turned into stories—were remarkably similar. And a couple of issues that were never publicly discussed were suddenly out in the open. Several of the teams' burning platforms uncovered some cross-functional issues that had not previously been addressed.

When Tippeconnic's team told its story, the team members no longer had to make the case for change. It had been made for them by everyone else. They could celebrate the alignment and move on to a discussion about next steps.

"Taking everyone through this process was a very effective tool for laying out strategic direction," says Tippeconnic. "People could quickly relate to the stories and understand them. They came to their own conclusions about what needed to change and where to focus."

Using Storytelling to Compete on Clarity

A Message Map is one way to approach corporate storytelling. It's not the only way. There is nothing proprietary about using storytelling to organize and convey corporate strategy. Once you've learned the four-part structure, there are gazillions of ways to put the parts together.

"I habitually try to tell stories about how money gets made," says Mike O'Brien, president of ZoomTown.com, a subsidiary of Cincinnati Bell. "That comes from my dad."

"Once, I took a job and I didn't have a clue. I said to my dad, 'I'm excited, but I don't know anything about this business. How do I figure out how it works?' And he said, 'Get a hold of the checkbook. Figure out why money is coming into it and why money is being spent out of it. That will tell you how things work.' Stories can be very effective in taking complex ideas and bringing everybody to a common understanding."

University of Michigan professor Noel Tichy has used storytelling constructs to develop what he calls a "teachable point of view."

In a recent *Harvard Business Review* article, Tichy reviewed how companies like GE, PepsiCo, AlliedSignal, and Ford are using stories as a strategic tool. He believes it's the "antidote to the 'black box' in people's heads—the box that conceals the origins of good ideas and important insights."[2] Tichy gives three reasons why an easy-to-convey, teachable point of view works so well:

- **The process actually creates better leaders.** It provides the time to reflect and makes implicit knowledge explicit. Assumptions are questioned, refined, and changed.
- **The process creates speed and reach.** All leaders who have used this approach say it quickly develops shared mindset across the organization.
- **The process teaches leading by example.** Storytelling gives leaders an explicit body of knowledge to impart, and it helps them help everyone work smarter.

More and more, a baseline requirement of leaders is being able to organize their ideas, plans, and strategies for "teachable moments." Yearly strategies won't move into implementation unless they are one-page stories. (Tichy says two pages. But you get the point. More is not better.)

The Future of Storytelling Is Also Digital

John Seely Brown, director of Xerox's Palo Alto Research Center, reports, "We've developed a system called Eureka through which we capture knowledge as stories. It leverages the learning from both telling and listening to a story. When you know what a story does, it helps you interpret the context you are in."

Chicago-based Diamond Technology Partners had an interesting challenge during its first growth spurt. As the company grew from 20 people to 85 to several hundred, the employees wanted to understand the vision of the company principals. But the founding partners didn't have time for all that storytelling. So they took inspiration from the company's middle name and developed a cutting-edge techno-solution.

Sixteen of the company's executives were interviewed, producing 21 hours of raw video footage. The edited stories were loaded into a digital system. In all, 409 video clips, with an average length of 35 seconds, were created with over 6,000 hyperlinks between the clips.

All new hires could click their way though the corporate story.

Although the hyperlinks meant that every story was a unique experience (there was no defined beginning, middle, or end), the messages and ideas conveyed were always consistent. Because content got as much thought and attention as technology.

If all that hyperlinking has you longing for a good ole campfire story, the digital world has that too. Dana Atchley began his career learning to set type and print books by hand. Since the '60s, he has been exploring the frontiers where art meets technology. Atchley is the founder of the Digital Storytelling Festival and now creates digital stories for clients.

A typical Atchley story begins in the dark around a campfire. You hear his voice over the crackling and popping of the fire, but you can't see him. As the lights come up, you discover his campfire is inside a monitor. All his stories are visual and use multiple monitors. As the fire burns on, the stories become interactive. Just as when you watch an improvisation comedy troupe, you are drawn in by his ability to make any visual appear and respond to the flow of the conversation with the audience.

The technology of storytelling is changing daily. Tomorrow's strategic rollouts will be aided by wearable computers. But high-tech presentations are not what turns storytelling into a business tool.

Bringing It All Together

The art of storytelling has always been about the ability to connect, excite, and amaze. To explain a future that cannot be seen or to create clarity out of today's data smog.

The senior execs who "get it" understand that their story is not just spin or packaging. *The story is the list of what must get done.* In a world where the workforce controls what gets done through the choices they make, order doesn't come from governance or from cascaded plans. Bringing it all together is about the clarity of ideas—and having the ability to convey those ideas in day-to-day conversations.

Nobody has the time or ability to filter all the emails, voicemails, and countless meetings and match them against some corporate strategy or business plan. But stories are easy to grasp, store, and recall.

The list of what needs to be done is the story about the strategy, and we carry it inside our heads. Not the strategy itself. It's not even the top three or four measures of success.

That's because storytelling is a universal translator. It's like the Rosetta stone. It is the one filter people from finance, operations, technology, janitorial services, and the executive suite all have in common. Stories give the list of what needs to be done a personality, passion, meaning, and connection to the work we do.

John Seely Brown may have been speaking for himself when he

GETTING STARTED: THE BASICS

- Eventually, you will work on your one-page story, bringing it all together to make the complex clear. For now, don't go there. Instead...
- Do a "gap analysis" of your current story. Using the sidebar "How Storytelling Works as a Business Tool" on pages 102-103, examine your last communication of The Strategy. Then answer these questions:
  - How could you improve how you made the case for change?
  - How clear, concise, and short was this year's definition of success?
  - How often during the year have you reinforced it?
  - If you lined up a hundred people and asked them about their understanding of the strategy and the company's definition of success, would you be satisfied with the answers?
  - Since launching The Strategy, how often have you celebrated successes and failures?
  - Were those celebrations explicitly communicated as progress away from the need to change or towards the definition of success? (Was the link to The Strategy clear?)
- What you find in this analysis will quickly help you understand why so many associates believe there's no clarity and their list just seems to get longer and longer. Present your findings to the senior team.
- If your case is strong enough, they will champion the development of a one-page teachable point of view.

said: "The really good strategic planners I know always do it around telling stories. And the ones that I'm highly suspicious of are the ones who have the strategy emerge purely from the analytics."

But the sentiments are the difference between a great strategy and a strategy that gets implemented. People act when the story makes not only business sense but emotional sense.

GETTING STARTED: ADVANCED LEVEL

Let's say you are satisfied with how you have organized and delivered your strategic story. Here is a higher-level gap analysis also based on the sidebar on pages 102-103:

- **Conflict.** How many people know what to scan for to see tomorrow's burning platform? Too many companies have too few people thinking about tomorrow. How many people in your organization have "environmental scanning" tied to their compensation? Each year, how often do you engage your senior team in discovery of what the next big challenges are likely to be? Also, refer back to Chapter 3. Do you consider complexity and decisional overload to be burning platforms?

- **Transition.** Celebrating successes and failures: Are you happy with the number of celebrations? If there are too few, people won't see the connection between this year's efforts and next year's—which makes this a lot more than a "soft," cultural issue.

- **Climax.** Sure, you have a very sophisticated process for rolling up everyone's targets into a corporate definition of success. But how many of your execs can explain the roll-up in day-to-day conversations with any associate anywhere?

- **Close.** Sure, the execs are all aligned around the Mission/Vision/Values. But are their infrastructures? If you randomly selected a hundred people from the organization and asked how their tools, support, and training helped them work toward the Mission, would you be satisfied with the answers?

HOW STORYTELLING WORKS AS A BUSINESS TOOL

Although there are countless ways to get everyone focused on the corporate strategy, they all come down to two things: **(1)** Creating common meaning for the very few things that are most important this year; **(2)** through conversation, creating a shared purpose—an easy-to-understand context for making decisions in a complex world.

Great stories can convey any idea to anyone. But you need to understand how to structure a great story. If you know the

---

1. CONFLICT
THE BUSINESS CASE
FOR CHANGE

Without conflict or a protagonist, you do not have a story. In business, that means people need to be dissatisfied with the current way of doing things in order to do things a new way. Corporate America's biggest mistake: Senior management keeps selling its conclusions about why everyone in the company needs to change. In a story, the listener tolerates the storyteller's logic but forms his/her own conclusions. A successful case for change provides associates with useful data and trends (the same raw materials that senior management used) and encourages them to draw their own conclusions.

---

2. TRANSITION
CELEBRATING
SUCCESSES
AND FAILURES

All stories need transitions to move the listener along. In business, transitions occur when the company celebrates successes and examines lessons learned. These moments help everyone understand how far they've come or how they could improve. Very few companies celebrate success enough. Even fewer celebrate and promote the lessons they've learned. Result: Many changes sound like "flavors of the month" because the company is lousy at creating moments of transition. It's difficult for the average associate to see how all the changes are connected and moving the company forward.

structure, you can build strategies that also create common meaning and context. **(Even one gap in the structure is like a hole in a story. Your strategy just won't make sense to people.)**

If you take away anything from this chapter, make it those last two sentences. If your strategy isn't clear because there are gaps in your story, gaps in execution of your plan are *guaranteed.*

3. CLIMAX SUCCESS THIS YEAR	In a story, the climax is the moment of truth. In business, the climactic moment is when this year's measures of success are met. Overlaying the structure of a story on top of a strategic plan helps you see gaps that won't show up when strategies are structured in other ways. For example: 1. Can everyone in your company describe corporate, business unit, and team success? Storytelling structures help with this. Most strategic planning structures don't. 2. Even when senior execs know their top measures of success, few can finish this sentence when talking to any associate in the organization: "Here is what this measure means in what you do every day…" 3. Most performance management systems ignore the fact that the important stuff happens in conversations, not in plans or formal evaluations.
4. CLOSE MISSION, VISION, VALUES	People need to see what all their hard work is for. But beware of getting too good at communicating the Mission/Vision/Values at the cost of the tools, processes, and support everyone needs to unleash their full potential. Creating shared mindset is a wonderful thing, as long as the infrastructure keeps pace with the discussion of where everyone wants to go.

Simpler Companies

Are you designing smarter work?

A truly simpler company must start with the basics from the previous section. Half the discipline of simplicity happens one person at a time—in how you and your associates use each others' time and share what you know.

The other half is **what you build** to bring all that sharing into execution, decisiveness and agility.

Great companies execute. But simpler companies do one thing differently. They **work backwards** from what people need. They know that people will trust the corporate infrastructure to help them work smarter if the tools, processes and information are grounded in their needs. So simpler companies start at the front lines, where employees and customers meet, then work backwards into business needs.

This changes how we design work. Simpler companies are **"user centered."** They adapt to the needs of day-to-day decision makers. This shift may push some leaders out of their comfort zone. In the following chapters, you will learn how to start building a simpler infrastructure.

It is easy to recognize a simpler company. It's a place where people can trust the company to help them work smarter—where information and infrastructure are designed around the people who use them.

MIND-SHIFT

This section is about simpler
and smarter execution.
Shut the book now if you
expect that to mean simpler,
easier leadership.

Chapter 9

Simpler to Know

A strategy for working backwards

Opportunity is missed by most people because it is dressed in overalls
and looks like work.

Thomas Edison, user-centered inventor

Bob Glass tells great stories. Like how one of his company's
services got dubbed the Vomit Comet. (Glass is chief technology
Officer for Weaver Aerospace. Besides working on important advances,
like developing ways to deliver payloads into space for one-tenth the
current cost, Weaver has also gone Hollywood. In *Apollo 13,* for
example, the weightless scenes were provided by Glass' company.
They flew parabola loops in a jumbo jet to create brief moments of
weightlessness. You can guess how the nickname got started.)

Glass also spins great tales about the time he spent as head of
Human Factors Engineering at Sun, as well as similar positions at
Apple and Xerox.

But one of his best is about NASA during the early days of *Skylab.*
Glass was known as the space-walk guy for bringing ergonomic design
to how people worked in space. NASA's engineers built lots of stuff for
the walks, but the astronauts couldn't use the equipment by themselves,
says Glass. So NASA's solution was to build yet more tools the
astronauts could hold, which were then attached to the gadgets that
did the work.

"I said, 'Your customer is a person in a suit that's pressurized. Why
don't we quantify what he or she can do? How about measuring how
much they can move their fingers, their head, or rotate their body? Then
design hardware that is optimal for those movements.'"

After validating that underwater tests provided conditions similar to

CHAPTER PUNCHLINE

People have limitless capacity to work smarter.

As long as what you build is user centered.

kn

WORKFORCE TO EXECS

"We could work

so much smarter.

If only..."

w

THE MODEL FOR MAKING THINGS SIMPLER TO KNOW

Put yourself in the other person's shoes. Period.
In life, this is called common sense.
In selling, it is called customer focus.
And when designing information-based work, it is called being user-centered.

THE MODEL IN ACTION

E-commerce and call centers use this model. Tons of people — from techno-wonks and content experts to anthropologists—study how the customer wants and uses information. Every effort is made to design backwards from what the customer needs to make smart and easy decisions. And it's not just the info. The tools... the interfaces... the relationship... the entire experience is user centered and customized.

WHY MOST COMPANIES DON'T USE THE MODEL

1. Very few are as sophisticated in meeting the needs of knowledge workers as they are forced to be with customers.
2. Customizing to meet user needs means understanding and admitting how much control the workforce has in making day-to-day choices.
3. The myth that work complexity comes from "out there" is still pervasive. So most companies have not admitted "We have met the enemy and he is us."

outer space, Glass worked on the new designs. "We were trying to convince the senior executives to make changes in design. NASA could save time and money and didn't need additional tools if the designs were appropriate for the people doing the work."

When it was time to demonstrate the results, Pete Conrad, commander of the space station and the third person to walk on the moon, did color commentary for the press briefing. *Aviation Week*, NASA, as well as U.S. Navy and Air Force officials all believed that it would take 45 minutes to complete a particular task in the underwater tank. The astronauts were done in three and a half minutes. "We just designed for the people doing the work," concludes Glass.

Knowledge Workers Without Limits

Glass' design principles can be applied to all knowledge work. Whenever you work backwards from what people need—tailoring experiences to how they learn or helping them customize information to the way they need it—they work smarter. Your tools and processes can help them order, make sense of, and understand everything that demands their attention.

This means only half the responsibility for making the complex clear resides with your associates and depends on how well they share what they know. The other half is your responsibility: Start with user needs, and work backwards from there in order to create more clarity.

Most companies work hard to manage clarity from above. As a senior executive from one of the world's best performing companies said, "We are committed to putting the business strategy in simple and repeatable terms, and to creating common meaning for people to talk to one another." Any effort like this—involving creating shared mindset or context—will always be important.

But don't confuse this work with simplicity. When it comes to the kind of clarity that is truly empowering, where a person's only limit is his or her imagination, companies must be user centered. This means continually adapting to the needs of the day-to-day decision makers.

Making It Simpler to Work Smarter

The company adapts to the needs of day-to-day decision makers. Whoa. Some people just slammed the book shut. Too radical. Too much loss of control.

They can't conceive a business in which project leaders help create stretch goals for senior execs—because they know what it *really* takes to get customer focused. Or where forklift drivers and cashiers can have reports designed to *their* specs, not the way Corporate wants them designed. Or why someone would be held accountable for designing performance tools that *excite* people into asking for more data—because the tools follow entertainment and education principles.

Nor can they imagine that companies will think about respect in new ways. Simpler companies will ask questions such as "Do all of our tools respect people's time—is it easy for them to get what they need? And do we respect our associates enough to make it easy for them to come to their own conclusions about our strategy—even if that makes it harder for our senior execs to put 'corporate spin' on the message?"

For any leaders who are still reading, creating thoughtful design of infrastructure from the user's perspective is hard work. You may need to change what you measure, where you focus, how work is designed... even leadership's role.

Most likely, building a user-centered infrastructure will require a mind-shift. Some of the control over tools, processes and information flows will move to the people who use them.

If you are interested in creating a simpler company, the next page provides a strategy for making the shift. And Chapters 10–13 provide the details about what it will take to put the strategy into practice.

Pop Quiz Alert

Don't jump ahead just yet. Think of the remainder of this chapter as pre-work—short stories about different ways to be user centered. Each is followed by questions and ideas that need to be discussed if you are going to get simple.

The pre-work ends with a short quiz about how all these stories relate to the number one source of work complexity.

A Strategy for Simpler, Smarter Work

THE NEED The biggest barrier to working smarter is our ability to order, make sense of, and connect everything that demands our attention

Goal: To make it easier to work smarter — a lot easier.

THE FIVE DISCIPLINES OF SIMPLER COMPANIES	WHAT'S NEW	THE DETAILS YOU'LL NEED
1. **Building Trust with What You Build**	The medium (your infrastructure) is the message: Are you to be trusted to help people work smarter?	**Feels Simpler** Chapter 10
2. **Designing Content for Decision Making**	You will design information so it actually informs and is easy to use. You will also be improving the performance of information.	**Simpler to Use** Chapter 11
3. **Using Project Design to Make Informed Choices**	Few projects are truly governed by plans, budgets, and tracking. Project design is really about organizing choices.	**Simpler to Do** Chapter 12
4. **Designing Work for Easy Navigation**	You will make it simpler to succeed because it's easier to see all the connections.	**Simpler to Succeed** Chapter 13
5. **Prototyping the Future**	You will make it easy for three groups to change your infrastructure: Customer. Company. And the people who have to use the darn stuff.	Chapters 10-13: Each contains a prototyping sidebar.

REPORT FROM A CONTENT DESIGNER

"The question facing me was: How do we get from a mass of 15,000 patients and five years' worth of data to what will help physicians and patients know what's important?" This comes from John Yates, a doctor who heads one of Merck's clinical research efforts.

"Recognizing how difficult this is, I set up teams of experts," says Yates. "For example, we established the Scientific Communications Group. Their role is to go through all the data and prioritize it, synthesizing it to communicate supportable core messages about the drug we're producing and what it does. Of course, our approach has to be scientifically valid. Truth and accuracy in how we interpret data is an absolute at Merck."

Yates says he prefers to think of himself as a physician first. And that the process of working through all that data keeps the patient at the front of every Merck decision. Yates' communication team connects patient, drug, and physician information in ways that make it easier for execs to discuss the connections between patient needs and business strategies. Yates concludes, "I think Merck has progressed to a very systematic and process-oriented approach. Everybody has the same understanding of the goals and all the information they need to make decisions."

FOR DISCUSSION: Merck, and any company seeking FDA approval, must have disciplined processes for moving from collecting and processing massive amounts of data to making informed decisions. Nowadays, so must every company. That's how knowledge management was born. It was meant to help develop, capture, and share what information people need to make decisions.

But there is a dark side to this force. If you exclude consulting and technology firms, very few companies are building teams like Merck's Scientific Communications Group. Anyone can add information, but who is working backwards from the users' needs? Who is scanning for patterns and trends and building connections between ideas to make decision making simpler? Although unfettered collaboration among teammates has huge upsides, it also creates an amazing amount of clutter and noise.

Externally—in the world of e-commerce—the teams that create clarity and focus out of noise are called *infomediaries*. They are providers who create value solely by sorting, prioritizing, and synthesizing information so customers can come in, make a decision, and get out. Quickly and easily. E-commerce calls this a "frictionless transaction" because the design places a premium on the efficient use of customer time. Everything is user centered, focused on the people who need to use the information to make decisions.

Internally, most of Corporate America has yet to face this wake-up call. Your average front-line employee is doing the same amount of sorting, prioritizing, and sense-making as Dr. Yates' team. (Revisit Chapter 2: The top sources of work complexity all relate to cognitive overload and lack of clarity.)

If we are expecting smarter work from a diverse workforce—which includes the three-quarters of us who need additional skills or tools to find the critical among the clutter—we are going to need more infomediaries inside our companies. Business is going to have to do a lot more to make information useful to people.

THREE STORIES ABOUT BREAKING
KNOWLEDGE AND PERFORMANCE BARRIERS

The Gozinta Circle

John Cochran talks excitedly about his company's awesome performance management system. Cochran is CEO of FirstMerit, a community bank that operates mostly in Ohio.

"We are viewed as a high-performance organization," says Cochran. "Every year Gallup surveys our employees. 'I know what is expected of me in my work' consistently gets the highest scores. This is because one of our guiding principles is 'If you measure it, it moves.' In most cases, the measures go into a quarterly personal scorecard. In some, it's weekly. We are probably the best in our industry at customizing performance information in the scorecards to match individual needs."

"All that customizing is supported by our second great quality, coaching. We have 130 coaches who focus on 'How are we doing against expectations?' We put a tremendous amount of effort into training and developing coaches. Finally, our compensation system pays for performance against plan. Two thousand of our 3,200 employees are on a bonus system that tracks 80 different customer-focused numbers. The other 1,200 are support people. They can make up to 200 percent of their salary based on performance incentives."

"We call it the gozinta circle," says Cochran with a smile. "The business plan gozinta your individual performance plan, which gozinta your measurement, which gozinta your coaching, development, and rewards. All the customizing to individual needs boils down to one thing. We differentiate ourselves by executing very, very well. Every day, every one of our employees is focused on our strategy of building a relationship with our customers."

FOR DISCUSSION: A fully integrated performance management system—a gozinta circle—is how lots of companies simplify and focus the decisions made by associates. The list of what's important is tightly managed and measured.

But most of these measurement and management systems can't keep up with Internet time and constant change. If you are larger or less disciplined than FirstMerit, the engines behind these systems are probably stalling. Senior execs still get customized, timely, and useful information. Managers and employees don't—because it would be too complex for the company to get it to them.

Any company installing Enterprise Resource Planning (ERP) and Human Resource Information (HRI) systems knows this firsthand. They are part of the engine behind performance management. Yet, according to a 1999 GartnerGroup study of more than 1,300 companies in the United States and Europe:

- Senior execs regard ERP projects as dangerously prone to implementation failure
- Failures have little to do with technology. The causes are mostly
  - Uncommitted sponsors
  - Unrealistic expectations
  - Inexperienced project teams
  - Unwillingness to commit sufficient resources

The bottom line is that most of the people in these companies aren't getting the feedback or information they need when they need it, how they need it.

At most companies, performance management isn't even pretending to be user centered. And members of the workforce aren't trusting the corporate infrastructure to help them work smarter. If you have a performance management system and you want it to be trusted, it must provide real-time and customized feedback to *100 percent* of your associates.

To get there, you will need to smash a huge barrier to working smarter.

The Barrier Between Knowledge and Performance Systems

Dave Browne, CEO of LensCrafters, is focused on this challenge. As described in Chapter 4, he firmly believes senior management's role is to help synthesize and sort information. His COO is personally charged with coordinating what goes to the LensCrafters stores each week. Reducing clutter is an executive suite accountability. But Browne says the biggest value is what happens next.

"If you want to increase capacity for knowledge work, empowerment becomes customization. We spend a lot of energy on this," says Browne, "because it's how we add value to customer focus. We know what customer data is most important to results. We capture it in ways that are best for the company. But then we give people tools so they can rearrange anything in the database."

"They set their own deviation parameters. They can set their own deviation reporting. They do whatever they need to do to run each store. We are not so presumptuous as to say we have a given format that everybody uses and likes. I've designed the reports I need to run the company. But we have built the database in such a way that anything inside can be tailored to many uses."

Browne concludes, "Having data in the form that people can use it to act is essential. This way, they can quickly see patterns and trends in their own work. Giving people the flexibility to create actionable formats is how we've approached it." LensCrafters store managers *design* what they need to work smarter. They—not Corporate—are in control of how best to organize and use performance data.

A similar example comes from Kent Greenes, formerly of BP Amoco. While he was their chief knowledge officer, he stressed: "The criteria we use to organize knowledge are around very real business needs plus the needs of the individual. This demands transparent data flows—meaning that anybody can dip into corporate information and create the views they need. The profit centers and the people doing the work need to be able to organize it to meet their needs."

FOR DISCUSSION: Unfortunately, Browne and Greenes are describing a way of working that is radical for much of Corporate America. They have removed the artificial boundary between knowledge and performance systems. In their companies, individuals can easily customize corporate data any way *they* need it.

Working smarter means more than creating collaborative workspaces—places where people can customize their own conversations and information. That's a no-risk, high-gain form of empowerment: Associates are in charge of learning. Headquarters is in charge of execution.

Working smarter means that any and all corporate data relevant to an individual's work should be available in formats that can be customized. Everyone in your organization should be able to take what is inside

- The business model
- Customer data
- The business plan
- The strategic plan
- Performance data
- Competitive data

and customize whatever is relevant to his or her work. And not just within one tool or one report. It should be a lot easier, let's say, for a call center rep to customize and compare any data you have on the marketplace, his own performance, and what's in the business plan. If it's easy enough, he could create his own aha's instead of waiting for some supervisor to explain why things are changing again.

In a few situations, confidentiality will create limitations. But you cannot sidestep this approach. If your goal is simplicity, making all corporate data available in formats that can be customized is a must. It provides people a quick means of seeing patterns, connections, and all the important trends.

When you make it easy for people to jump between knowledge and performance systems, you make a huge leap in smartness. People get half of what they need to make decisions from collaboration. The other half comes from what the business is tracking. Make it complicated to see all the connections between the two, and associates will always depend on you to create clarity for them.

"Tailoring information and work experiences is all about creating a **learner-centered environment.** Information is indexed for the task they need to do. And they get to change it around according to their own information literacy."

DR. SUSAN LAND, Assistant Professor, Instructional Systems, Penn State

"A major part of having a collaborative environment is getting people the information the way they need to see it."

GEORGE POR
Founder and
Senior Consultant
Community
Intelligence Labs

"All the academic and business research I've done shows one undeniable factor. Learning environments **that do not fit** an individual's learning style and process **are not used.**"

RICHARD DURR, Senior Manager
Learning Strategies, Motorola

"There is no one right way, but there aren't a million ways either. We've done the social science research to observe people's decision-making habits. You've got to watch like an anthropologist would to see the patterns emerge."

CHRISTINE ALBERTINI
Research and
Development
Steelcase Furniture

Changing How You Ask Questions Changes How You Use Projects
Clement Mok is founder of Studio Archetype, a San Francisco-based
firm specializing in creating online experiences. Mok reports an
interesting learning that happened when his 140-person firm was
acquired by Sapient, a business consulting and technology firm.

"I'm now part of an organization with about 1,300 people. So we
had to formalize a lot of our people processes. What an eye-opener.
Sapient takes everyone through a boot camp program. The first week
is focused on the vision and mission. The next four to five weeks are
spent on facilitation: Role-playing and learning how to run meetings."

"This company has made facilitation a core competency. It's not
design or even smarter people. It's asking better questions. Every single
programmer, every designer, everybody is taught how to frame
discussions and have conversations. The business outcome is smarter
work. Every project is tighter because everyone is creating his or her
own clarity. People fully understand the choices to be made." Mok
closes with a simple "Wow!"

Some might say there is nothing new here. Sapient is just creating
better ways to collaborate. In fact, something bigger has happened. The
company has reinvented a primary way of organizing work—project
design.

FOR DISCUSSION: For any firm *without* an organization-wide ability to
ask better questions, project design is mostly about creating 'to do' lists
that can be tightly managed. The primary goal is organizing timelines,
budgets, measures, and the like.

Sapient and companies like it recognize that there's a more
important dimension to project design. A project is the exact place and
time where corporate, personal, team, and customer needs converge on
a manageable scale. All the trade-offs and decisions get debated at the
project level more than anywhere else. Project design is really about
organizing choices.

For example, when project teams see all those needs come together,
they discuss the following issues: How much are we willing to invest in
the project? Why would our associates or customers choose to use
whatever we are designing? Will senior execs have to change how they
lead to ensure the project's success? etc.

These nuances are lost on many companies. It's a shame, because
such oversights almost always bite them in the butt. The most common

reason, by far, for implementation failure is lack of clarity or agreement on choices and behaviors. (Remember the main reasons ERP projects fail: Uncommitted sponsors, unrealistic expectations, inexperienced project teams, unwillingness to commit sufficient resources—all relate to choices project team members make or don't make.)

So the companies that get simple will recognize that some of the most important questions and discussions about choices come up when projects are being designed. They will find ways to tap into everything that project teams learn about making choices. And they will aggressively use what they've learned to change how leaders, managers, and associates discuss the choices they face.

HOW DO YOU DESIGN A CHANGING FUTURE FROM THE USER'S PERSPECTIVE?

Jim Dixon is head of technology and operations for Bank of America. Mergers brought the number of associates in his group to 45,000. And since technology is so critical to the banking industry, he's in charge of a $5 billion budget.

Dixon explains one of the tools his group used to help build a new, post-merger infrastructure. "We visualized our business model. The strategy was just too far from the work that needed to be done. So we illustrated all the layers of what we're building: A customer-driven structure—processes, workflow, governance, the whole thing." Dixon's goal was to take a jigsaw puzzle—the structures and inner workings of the new business model—and create a complete, comprehensible picture.

Design firms have a name for Dixon's visualization. They call it a prototype. It's the representation of something that does not yet exist. Architects, product designers, and software developers have always used prototypes as tools to engage their clients before moving into execution. Prototypes make it easier for everyone involved to react to ideas and change things before they are built.

While we can dive deep into all the details," Dixon continued, "the overview makes it clear that everything comes down to three customer activities: Inquire, Buy, and Use. We simplified everything in the model to address what customers want [Inquire], the decisions they'll make [Buy], and the actions they'll take [Use]."

"Besides being a great way of engaging people," says Dixon, "this process has helped everyone talk about all the connections we have to create. For example, we paired some internal folks with an outside firm to help redesign our payment system. The team began its recommendation by describing how it fit within the business model and explaining which processes we'd have to change because they were linked to the payment system."

"In complex operating environments, if you can visualize the business model, you change conversations and how questions get asked. That changes and simplifies execution," concludes Dixon.

FOR DISCUSSION: Especially in situations like Dixon's, where a merger completely changed the puzzle, prototypes create a clear picture of the goal. And, just as important, they make it easier for everyone involved to provide feedback and make changes.

But, like content design, prototyping has a dark side. Most companies seek associate feedback on their infrastructure only once a redesign team has been formed. Put more bluntly: Associate involvement in designing corporate infrastructures is not desired unless asked for. Most companies make it hard for the average user to comment on, or change, corporate-built stuff. In these companies, if front-line people have ideas for changing tools, processes, or information flows—all in the name of customer focus and business results—they have to wait for senior execs to sponsor a redesign.

In a world that changes by the minute, this approach to infrastructure design is creating massive amounts of complexity for our workforce. Companies that are seeking simplicity will do something about this.

They will start designing their infrastructure according to the three guiding principles of prototyping:

1. Make it easy for people to react to structures before they are in place
2. Make it easy for people to change what you are building by providing continual feedback
3. Get faster and faster at numbers 1 and 2 (known as "rapid prototyping")

Lots of companies follow these principles *externally,* with customers.

For example, all software is developed this way. Before a product is officially released, customers have made substantial changes and improvements. And as soon as version 1.0 is released, customers are already contributing to 2.0.

Simpler companies will bring this idea inside the organization. Fewer redesign teams will be needed because the company will make it easier for everyone to continually adapt and tweak the systems. Company leaders will know that the best way to become user centered is to let the people doing the work have a continuous role in developing the infrastructure. Redesign will happen daily. And if a major redesign is needed, the first call will come from the middle of the organization, not the top.

Simpler companies will make it easy for three groups to change their infrastructure: Customers. The Company. And the people who have to use the darn stuff. Prototyping is how these firms will design a changing, unknown, future from the user's perspective.

THE DAILY MIRACLE WORKER

Currently, how are most companies trying to be user centered? They hire as many Kathleen Bakers as possible.

"We work hard at staying focused and creating useful team experiences," says Baker, an organizational design manager for Hewlett-Packard. "HP has built a global manufacturing and distribution network. So my team is all over the place, literally. We are virtual— rarely in the same place together. So we work hard at being collaborative over the phone. We've got to create the same experiences as if we were always in the same facility together."

Baker represents Corporate America's best approach to people development. She is someone who uses time effectively while being pulled in multiple directions. And she's great at creating just-in-time clarity for her team. Yet she says that what she does is definitely not rocket science. "It just takes discipline and commitment. We're religious about project updates and sharing performance information. But we try to keep them to email. That way, we can keep phone time sacred for learning, working, and creating as a team."

FOR DISCUSSION: Even in this section—dedicated to changing your infrastructure—it is important to mention the Kathleen Bakers of the world, because any strategy for making knowledge work simpler revolves around people. Unfortunately, as we've seen in previous chapters, many managers and project leaders are not as skilled or as disciplined as Baker in finding the critical among the clutter. As a result, everyone they touch gets swamped with too many choices, too much information that isn't useful.

If your goal is to maximize the potential of every individual in a diverse workforce, part of your people development strategy must include making it easier for associates to customize what they need, and easier for them to change the things now controlled by Corporate. After all, the Kathleen Bakers can't help everybody all the time.

The Simpler-To-Be-Smarter Quiz

You've read several stories about working smarter by being user centered. Each raised challenges you may face and showed how discussions have to change if you are to get simple. Time for a pop quiz:

1. Is everyone in your organization using most of his or her capacity to work smarter?
2. Do you currently have a strategy to create simpler, smarter work?

If you looked at any of the stories and said, "We don't do that," or if you looked at any of the challenges raised in this chapter and said, "We're not talking about that," the answer to both questions is probably: No.

A strategy for creating an environment where every person can work smarter includes everything you just read. It looks at your entire company as an integrated information space. It's all about the convergence of people development, information development, and technology.

Road Trip: Flip back to the table on page 29 in Chapter 2. The workforce is emphatic: Lack of integration is their number one source of work complexity. But they define it differently than leaders do. Leadership is focused on governance and coordination.

The workforce defines integration as: Right information in the right way, right quality, right amount, right time so they can make decisions that lead to success.

The Five Disciplines of Simpler Companies

Having a strategy for creating simpler, smarter work is about doing what it takes to satisfy the workforce view of integration. This means working backwards from their needs in five ways:

1. Build trust with what you build. Keep doing everything you've been doing to build trust. But also listen to Marshall McLuhan. The medium (your infrastructure) is your message. In a world of infinite choices, inability to customize tools, information, and experiences to individual needs sends a message: "Don't trust us to help you work smarter."

It's as if NASA refused to work backwards from the needs of the astronauts, telling them, "Hey guys, we built the people systems to get the best astronauts. And we designed the information so Mission Control could maintain control. And we designed the technology to get you up there and back. But if anything gets out of our control, it's your job to integrate all that, real-time, while you're walking around up there. OK?"

What astronauts would trust NASA with their lives? If you're not customizing to meet people's needs, don't expect a lot of trust in corporate-built stuff. (See Chapter 10 for ways to build trust.)

2. Design content for decision making. Go back to the dots and the funnel on pages 34-35. If the information that people use to make choices wasn't designed backwards—based on what they need—their experience looks more like the dots than the funnel. (See Chapter 11 for how to change this.)

3. Use project design to make informed choices. Few successful projects are truly governed by plans, budgets, and progress reports. If the projects involve behavioral change and working smarter, project design is mostly about discussing and organizing choices. Simpler companies know this and will push what they learn from project design teams—especially the ideas that upset the status quo—into the fabric of the organization. (See Chapter 12.)

4. Design work for easy navigation. To the people trying to get work done, there is no boundary between their performance and the

WHAT'S AN INFORMATION SPACE?

Throughout this section, you will be asked to look at your infrastructure the way the workforce sees it. What matters most is whether they get what they need to work smarter, when they need it, how they need it. When they are trying to work smarter, they don't see business units, enterprise software, intranets, leaders or managers or teammates, governance, processes, performance tools, or business plans. (Or anything else you might list.)

What they see is your information space—how all those things do, or do not, come together so they can get stuff done. If you want to get simple, you need to start looking at things through their eyes.

"If we're going to make things simpler without making them stupid, it's all about the process of sorting and prioritizing our thinking."

JESSICA LIPNACK, author of *Virtual Teams*

collaborative information that is available to them. Wipe it out. Also, if your merged knowledge system isn't easy to navigate—get in, get what you need to make a decision, and get out—you are greatly reducing the number of people who will find your knowledge system valuable. If you focus on navigation, you will make it simpler for people to succeed, because it will be easier for them to see how everything connects. (See Chapter 13.)

5. Prototype the future. The only way you can keep up with massive changes happening at breakneck speed *and* reduce work complexity is if you make it easier for the average associate to adapt some of your tools, processes, and information flows to the way he or she needs to use them. Simpler companies will do this by giving people daily opportunities to tweak and adjust their infrastructure. (See sidebars in Chapters 10–13 for ways to get started and things to think about.)

Your First Decision

Some pages ago, we began the journey toward a simpler company by talking about astronauts and outer space. We close with a look at the final frontier of empowerment.

In the 1960s theoretical biologist Stuart Kauffman pushed the limits of thinking by exploring the science of complexity. You've encountered him several times in this book. He coined the phrase "order for free." His idea, simply put: Complex systems (like companies) can't be controlled (with things like strategies, plans, and compensation schemes). Systems create their own order when you focus on relationships and the exchange of information.

Since Kauffman, many scientists and thought leaders have been working on ways to apply his ideas to business. Recently the consulting firm Ernst & Young brought together some of these pioneers at a conference titled "The Adaptive Enterprise."

Cool stuff is already happening. The marriage of this new science and technology is creating new ways to arrange stores according to buying habits, help the U.S. Marines organize troops, help Southwest Airlines reduce cargo handling by up to 70 percent without compromising on-time delivery.

That cool stuff, however, is happening *externally*, in the world of customers and competition. It's time to look inward, and time to make your first decision about building a simpler company.

The adaptive enterprise begins at home. With your associates. If you want knowledge workers without limits, you'll need to continually adapt to the needs of these day-to-day decision makers. Whatever you build must be user centered in the exchange of information and how you create relationships between ideas and people.

First decision: Can you afford *not to* be user centered?

SIMPLE NOTES

This is the first place in the book where senior execs are being asked to commit to changes in infrastructure, tools, and processes. There is no avoiding the obvious. Implementing a strategy for simpler, smarter work will be hard and may change some of your current plans. There are three reasons that doing so is worthwhile:

- Execution will be simpler, faster, easier—driving growth and profitability.
- Associates will work smarter—driving everything.
- Simplicity heightens associate accountability. Implicit in the many mentions of "user-centered" are higher expectations.

GETTING STARTED

- Introspection:
  - Have you had any new aha's? Did this chapter raise any new or different ways of thinking about smarter work?
  - How much do you *really* trust your associates? Some leaders will believe the strategy proposed in this chapter grants workers too much empowerment and leaders not enough control. Although there is no right or wrong answer, not articulating your senior team's position is destructive. Get it on the table, and make sure it is understood by all.
- Use page 112 as a template for working out your strategy. Then use the remaining chapters in this section to jump-start your discussions about how you'd fill in the template.

Chapter 10

Feels Simpler

Build trust with what you build

Be not deceived. Revolutions do not go backward.

Abraham Lincoln, student of human nature

How people feel is important. As Dr. Michael O'Brien said in Chapter 5, emotions will not be denied.

One of the all-time biggies is trust. Whenever a team or business grows larger than one person, trust becomes critical. We need to know that we can depend on each other, and that the company will create an environment in which we can thrive as individuals. Quick: Can you describe trust in the workplace five different ways?

Odds are your list includes at least one or two of these items:
- The business and my team are interested in me as an individual
- I can make a difference. My work contributes to the goal.
- Those around me have the same values, goals, and purpose I do
- I don't need to check my decisions with others
- I am treated fairly, the same as others, and have the same opportunities to contribute
- I can accept and give feedback openly
- Communication is open and timely
- I feel comfortable asking others to do better, and they can ask the same of me
- I can depend on the commitments people make to me, and they can depend on mine

Don't ever lose that list. It is universal, timeless, and very important.

CHAPTER PUNCHLINE

The workforce speaks out on the
employment contract

fe **l**

WORKFORCE TO EXECS

"Let's talk about what we
need to work smarter."

THE MODEL FOR COMPANIES THAT FEEL SIMPLER

Infrastructure, not just dialogue, is part of a two-way relationship. Tools, processes, and information flows change as much to meet users' needs as they do to meet customers' and the company's needs.

THE MODEL IN ACTION

Except for very small or very high tech companies, few practice this model internally, with associates. Externally, a great example is e-commerce.
The longer a customer has a relationship with a company, the more the relationship and information flow adapts to the customer's needs.
The customer tracks the experience in three ways:
1. Navigation: Easy to get in, make decisions, get out
2. Fulfillment: Getting exactly what is needed, how and when it is wanted
3. Time: Total respect for time and attention

WHY MOST COMPANIES DON'T USE THE MODEL

Duh.
Lack of massive bottom-up pressure. Boomers are the one-way TV generation. Although all of them use computers at work, few were raised on being in charge of total information experiences. Gen-Xers are smashing the old models, but statistically there aren't enough of them to force wide-scale changes in the corporate infrastructures of most businesses.

The New Lens

Something is about to happen. Something that has never occurred before, that will add a completely new dimension to that list: Associates will also want to know whether they can trust your tools, processes, and information flows to help them work smarter. If getting what they need to do their best doesn't feel simple, trust will plummet.

As this book first rolls off the press, the oldest of the Net Generation is joining the job market. Right behind them are 80 million peers, the sons and daughters of baby boomers. This population—also known as Gen Y, Echo Boomers, or the Millennium Generation—includes kids who are now playing with digital toys at the age of three. They represent the largest surge in the U.S. workforce since 72 million boomers hit the market.

They have been called the generation that must be reckoned with. Net Geners—incorrectly labeled indifferent, more correctly called independent—have new ideas about what it should feel like to work for you. They want to know they can trust what you are building. And they will force their definition of trust into the employment contract.

Revolutions Do Not Go Backwards

For the first time ever, business is hiring a workforce that grew up on mass-market, user-centered, interactive experiences. The same revolution that is creating your productivity gains also trained an entire generation in what information experiences should feel like. Simpler companies understand that many of their new hires have done lots of shopping for clothes, movie tickets, and books online. Some have even bought their first car and done grocery shopping and dry cleaning online.

In some ways, it doesn't matter whether their experiences involved buying things, doing high-level research, or playing *Doom, Riven,* or *Fast ForWord.* Before they join your team, many will have already spent a lifetime navigating information spaces. Their experiences may even help you address some literacy issues (see Chapters 2 and 3). You don't have to be an A student to know the amazing things a hyperlinked environment can do.

The experiences also raised expectations. Not only will Net Geners seek order through clarity and ease of use; that's how they will define environments they'll trust.

So What?

The next few pages detail what it will take for Net Geners to trust your infrastructure. If you hear anything similar from your associates, listen carefully. Your new hires are laying down terms for their employment contract.

They will stay, or walk, based on how you work backwards from their needs—for the same reasons you picked up this book. Simplicity is power. They want to work smarter, more easily. Like you, simplicity is also about their joy, passion, and work/life balance.

But there is one thing that separates this group from anyone older than their early twenties: Net Geners will seek simplicity by questioning what you build. Unlike any generation before, they will not join your team with the assumption that infrastructure is the domain of senior management. The Net, as we know it, was built in their lifetime. And not a single senior executive approved or supervised it.

They will look for an equal partnership in building what it takes for them to work smarter.

The New Workforce Speaks Out

As we walked the halls of Sharon High School outside of Boston, teacher and department chair John Brande shared a great story. A recent grad, David Karelitz, had a unique job while at Sharon High. He helped program and operate the New England Patriots' computerized scoreboard at Foxboro Stadium.

I met 16 of Karelitz's friends and peers (some of the people who will or will not trust what you're now building). I asked them what was important to them and how that might affect the business world.

Here are some high-school juniors and seniors **on Internet-type technologies:**

Drew Baglino,18: "The biggest plus and the biggest minus is finding what you need. If you have a very specific need, like getting a CD, you can get it easily, quickly. But if you need to learn, it's too sporadic, too strained, too much work. Until that changes, I'll use it as a utility. I go home, log on, listen to classical music from San Francisco. It's a happy thing for me."

Mike Liu,16: "To me, technology is just a tool. The Internet is just a hybrid of all the other media out there. It's another way to deliver information from point to point that's faster and more accessible."

Becca Sendker,17: "The biggest minus is knowing what you're looking for. If I had all the time in the world, I'd probably be on the Internet more. I really only use it for email, which I love because it's so easy. But I also think the Net makes some things too easy. It's promoting the dumbing down of our generation. It can be easy to forget that it's not about typing in *Hamlet* and finding the Cliff Notes."

Rebecca Deutsch,17: "The little time I do have, I don't want to spend on something computer related. I want to spend it with friends."

On the pluses and minuses of project teams:

Marc Wayshak, 17: "I went to business camp two summers ago. [Author's note: Reread that sentence and look at his age!] Business leaders said their biggest concern was knowing who to hire and who would work well with whom. When you have a team, you need to build a balanced group. And you need a facilitator who can put everyone's ideas together to create synergy."

Drew Baglino: "I'm not looking forward to a business world where groups dominate. I listen to my dad, and so many of the teams are mandated. It's not like you have the time to get to know each other."

Laura Brown, 17: "When the group works well, you work faster and better. My friend Becca made me work better. I wasn't capable of doing certain thinking on my own, but after listening to her ideas, mine were better."

On the skills Net Geners will need as they join the workforce:

Doug Levy, 18: "One of the most important things will be people who can organize their thoughts and put them together in an understandable format. People who can present their ideas to widespread and diverse groups."

Rebecca Deutsch: "You need to be able to teach and learn well. Because you need to get new ideas quickly and then convey your knowledge and help others learn."

Jake Garber,17: "Patience and interpersonal skills. Most of the work will be in groups."

Marc Wayshak: "You have to be able to communicate. And listen. A lot of people have difficulty listening. Including myself."

After a lengthy and wondrous conversation, I asked the group for help. If they were the designers, what would be most important in the information space they would build? The criteria I gave them: First, practicality. Second, it must include both people and digital approaches. And, most important, that they'd trust this environment to help them work smarter. They narrowed their list to three things:

1. **Navigation:** The information space should be easy to navigate and get around. It should be easy for everyone to find what they need to work smarter. And easy to see the connections between different ideas, people, and information.

2. **Right Quality, Right Way, at the Right Time:** Even the seasoned Net surfers among them said there was too much noise and clutter to cut through. If they were going to trust this environment to help them work smarter, the information space would have to be very good at getting them what they need, when they need it.

3. **Their Time Is Respected and Valued:** The system, whether it was face-to-face or online, would have to place a high value on their time. This meant learning from the user and continually shortening the time needed to get things done. Systems should also be designed based on what they wanted to accomplish. (Working backwards from their needs.)

Jenny Mae Kho, 17, provided an eloquent summary: "In the end, we're all human. It comes down to basic human nature. We need to pay attention to the way people connect and how they need things."

A Pattern Emerges

The more Net Geners I met, the more those three elements of trust kept coming up.

From recent grads of Drew University:

Stacy Levy: "We all have ten million things to do. We're all on overload. How my time is used is a big factor in trust."

Chris Grygo: "The ability to deal with ambiguity has a lot to do with these issues. Many people have lower tolerances for ambiguity. Trust happens when information sharing and navigation account for that."

Or from Northern Illinois University business majors:

Aaron Miller: "One thing is not changed by the Net. There is still a lot of subjective work—trying to pull all the information together and knowing what to trust to help you work smarter."

Or from Rutgers University marketing majors:

Michelle DiGiulio: "It is so critical to be able to present information in ways people need it. Which means both making it easy to navigate and delivering useful information..."

Connie Burman completed the point: "...Otherwise, why should they trust the information? Your audience is looking at you wondering 'What am I going to get out of this?'"

Both online and in person, I met Net Geners from over three dozen schools with different backgrounds and interests. In many ways, they were no different from every previous generation. They wanted to contribute in meaningful ways and make a difference.

The difference emerged when we discussed trust. In addition to the usual ideas—shared purpose and values, teamwork, etc.—they equated trust with the utility and efficiency of their information experience. They blurred the boundaries between technology, information design, and face-to-face communication. What mattered was the quality of the total experience.

Trust Confirmed

I could have saved myself a lot of time had I first checked with Clement Mok, chief creative officer of Sapient. His firm just completed a six-month research project on trust within information spaces. And the results were identical to what I heard at Sharon High.

"We started by focusing on online security," says Mok. "As it turned out, what we found is much larger. We found three meta-categories for information space trust:

1. **Navigation**
2. **Fulfillment**
3. **Time**

There are 28 subcategories within those three."

Mok continued, "Here's one example of how it works. Brand trust is important whether you are in e-commerce or based in the dirtworld. If you are an e-commerce start-up and you don't have a known brand, why should people trust you? One way to build a lot of brand equity very quickly is to have clarity of purpose and have the navigation be incredibly easy to use. If the navigation is strong and simple, it makes it easy to explore and compare purchasing options. Easy-to-compare information builds trust in any decision-making situation."

"That's the first part," says Mok. "You also need to be able to complete the fulfillment process in a time that matches expectations.

"Today's kids are much better at sense-making, improvising, and figuring things out during play than most mid- and senior managers. **We've got to start thinking** about the content and tools that will let them do that."

JOHN SEELY BROWN, Chief Scientist, Xerox Corporation, Director, Xerox PARC

"In the extended e-enterprise, we need to apply the same standards and principles internally as we do with customers."

PEHONG CHEN
President, BroadVision
(an e-commerce
technology firm)

"Just because I have access to everything, doesn't mean I need it. I feel better about not having to see everything. I try to find sources I can trust—both in people and in sites. Being able to easily zoom in and out from the larger picture also has a lot to do with trust."

TOMOKO ICHIKAWA, Information Designer
The Doblin Group

"Most of this is basic. It's all about what makes human beings tick. You can look at product innovation, operational excellence, everything. But the real competitive advantage comes down to people and earning their trust every day."

BILL HAMMAN, President
Education Division
Sodexho Marriott Services

We've seen companies following the guidelines within navigation, fulfillment, and time make huge leaps in brand trust."

But are these areas just as important internally? "Absolutely. Applied internally, we're talking knowledge management and communication. Navigation is how quickly they can find and get the information they need. Fulfillment is right quality, right amount, in the way the employee needs it. And time is when they need it. No extra steps, clicks, meetings, or hassles."

Mok concluded, "Any company that tracks and works on improving these three areas will see employee trust shoot way up."

Trust Is Power

Trust has always been important. But how often is it truly urgent? Usually just in crisis situations. No longer, and there are two reasons why:

- Net Geners will hike it to urgent and keep it there. They'll be looking for tools, processes, and structures they can trust to respond to their needs. If you don't build that way, they won't come. For those who do join your team, they'll continually evaluate whether your infrastructure is helping them work smarter.
- If your firm is like most, you've been misdiagnosing trust problems for years. Go back to Chapter 2 and read how choice overload has been wrongly labeled as "resistance to change." Lots of pre-boomers, boomers, and Gen Xers do not believe that your infrastructure can help them work smart enough, fast enough. This lack of trust has existed for a long time. The Net Geners, however, will make sure misdiagnoses no longer occur. Their numbers will be large enough and they will be impatient enough to be in-your-face about it.

Trust is no longer just a social contract. Beginning with the Net Geners, it's what they will require of you in their employment contract. They will ask whether they can trust you to help them work smarter. And they will track what you build on three fronts: navigation, fulfillment, and time.

The good news (for those who wish all of this would go away) is that it will take a few years for Net Geners to reach critical mass. Some companies won't face this reality until around 2010. The bad news is that if you wait that long, you'll be about 20 years behind.

Where to Start

First, where *not* to start. Do NOT focus on technology, data, or things. Please don't go to your techno-wonks. Focus on people. Trust is about the relationship you have with your workforce.

There is a name for building trust with what you build. "We call it a learning relationship," says Don Peppers, coauthor of *Enterprise One to One*. "If you're an e-commerce customer, the more you order from a company, the more they learn about your needs. They are able to tailor the experience to you. Changing how you order. Changing what they offer. Trust is built by the willingness to be completely user centered. Although most advances have been made with customers, the same principles apply internally."

Pepper's point is that this is not just about technology, and it's more universal than e-commerce. It's what the workforce will expect from a relationship with your company.

As we said in the previous chapter, the place to start is senior management's commitment to build tools, information, and experiences that are user centered. You need to decide whether you trust your associates enough to let their decision-making needs guide what you build.

PROTOTYPING A COMPANY THAT FEELS SIMPLER

Trust is no longer just a social contract. If it doesn't feel simple enough for people to get what they need to do their best, trust will plummet. Although there are no right or wrong ways to build

COMMON SENIOR EXEC COMMUNICATION	A NEW KIND OF RESPONSE	MODEL CITED
We have a new strategy. Everyone needs to rally around it.	**Uh-uh.** Your definition of success is unclear, and you haven't made a compelling case for change. Why don't you come back to us when you can defend the strategy?	**Presidential press conference:** Grilling a commander in chief about putting lives on the line for a noble cause.
We need to restructure to meet the needs of the marketplace. As of today, all our business units are new.	**Uh-uh.** Lots of packaging, no meat. Why don't you come back when the design teams know how this will affect real work?	**Where's the beef?** Working smarter means pushing back on anything that wastes time and attention.
	When you do come back— if your goal is to be smarter, faster—we'll need to see simulations of how restructuring changes our roles and what is important.	**Computer modeling**

"Clutter stops you from doing breakthrough thinking. Anything that helps you organize your thinking is going to take you to a higher level, get you to ask bigger questions."
DON WINKLER, Chairman and CEO, Ford Motor Credit Company

trust with what you build, the workforce will insist on the right to question and change tools, information, and experiences. Are you prepared for this kind of exchange?

COMMON SENIOR EXEC COMMUNICATION	A NEW KIND OF RESPONSE	MODEL CITED
We have a process for selecting and developing **high-potential future leaders** (HI-Po's).	**Too exclusive.** How about everybody in the company voting for Hi-Po's? Why don't we elect them for two-year terms of focused development, and our 360° feedback will determine whether or not each Hi-Po's term is renewed?	**Democratic governance**
We need a new **customer-focused process.** All that matters is the customer.	Great! But if your tools aren't designed around our needs as we interact with customers, we all lose. **Do you agree that user-centered** design is now important? If not, we, the design team, will go work for the competition.	**Free-market contracting**
We just merged with another company. We're **integrating the two IT platforms.**	**Too complicated and slow.** (And you'll do it all again with the next merger.) Why don't we build an open-source operating platform? A nonproprietary system would make it cheaper, quicker, and easier to merge and change.	**Linux operating system**

Chapter 11

Simpler to Use

Designing content for decision making

The act of arranging information becomes an act of insight.

Edward Tufte, Professor of Information Design and Statistical Evidence, Yale University

Of all the ways to create a simpler company, why is it important to worry about content—what people use to make decisions? That doesn't sound sexy or strategic, does it?

To discover why, try this exercise: (1) Turn the book upside down and point it at a mirror. (2) Look in the mirror. (3) Try to read this paragraph in less than six seconds.

You just experienced what it feels like to make quick decisions using what most companies provide for the task. Everything you needed was right in front of you, but it was organized to defeat your best effort.

In this exercise, your main focus was trying to use the words. That's what people who are trying to work smarter care about: "Has it been organized, filtered, screened, blessed, prioritized, or whatevered the way I need it to be so I can get stuff done?" The way we organize ideas on paper, online, and in discussions can radically change the productivity of knowledge work. For better or worse.

That's why content design becomes important. You can still be in a fog when surrounded by *data*bases, *information* systems, *knowledge* sharing, *learning* environments, and people full of *wisdom*. If these things aren't user centered—designed for what you need to get done— you probably don't have the time to use them effectively.

Think of content as datainformationknowledgelearningwisdom that has been organized for a specific use, decision, or conversation. For all those things to become content, someone has to consciously design them to be useful.

CHAPTER PUNCHLINE

It's all noise…until you focus on
what the person will use it for.

WORKFORCE TO EXECS

"Is anybody focused on
making this stuff useful?"

MODELS OF MAKING THINGS SIMPLER TO USE

- The signage system at the Louvre
- FedEx online tracking
- Map of the London Underground (circa 1932)
- *How Things Work,* by David Macaulay
- *USA Today*
- *Woman's Body,* by the Diagram Group: A Braille medical reference for blind Japanese women

THE MODEL IN ACTION

Look around. The model is everywhere you go as a *consumer.* At the e-commerce sites you love, in the CD-ROM you bought for your niece, at the concierge desk of your favorite hotel. Whenever other companies view you as a consumer of information, they focus on what you will use it for.

WHY THIS IS A LOW PRIORITY FOR MOST COMPANIES

It's all about assumptions. If you begin with the assumption that management tools (strategies, budgets, business units, processes, etc.) focus and structure people's choices, all your design time will go into these things. But if you believe that—even with great management tools—everyone is in choice and info overload, you invest in design differently. You spend a lot more energy on the content people use to make their everyday decisions.

Richard Saul Wurman knows this better than most of us. Wurman is obsessed with making the complex clear. He has authored more than 65 books on topics he wanted to better understand. He is also founder of the TED conferences, once-a-year confabs focused on the convergence of technology, entertainment, and design.

To Wurman, content design is about creating understanding. "Most organizations are still in the information collection, storage, and transmission business. What's most important is being in the understanding business. That means making things comprehensible. Design is about improving the performance of information—making sure it *informs* someone about something."

Wurman's passion for clarity shows in everything he does. About the same time this book is published, he will be shipping an atlas titled *Understanding*, which he plans to distribute for the cost of production and mailing. His goal in the atlas is to examine "the 600 or 700 questions fundamental to all Americans" in such areas as health care, education, and business. "Because it is designed based on how people ask questions, maybe they will find they can ask better questions," concludes Wurman.

So What?

When content is thoughtfully designed—from the user's perspective— the conversations and the questions change. Guess what: Lots of companies are preventing associates from working smarter and creating their own clarity.

At most companies, hardly anyone is working backwards from the users' needs on;

- Screen interfaces
- Customer reports
- Database structures
- Data-mining output
- Performance reports
- Workflow representations
- Information hierarchies
- Project status reports
- Community yellow pages...

...and countless other ways of organizing content for decision-making. This means associates have to work way too hard to find the one nugget they need. Or to understand what is being asked of them. Or to ask new and different questions.

At most companies, the discipline of designing content for decision making stinks.

Not only does a lot of corporate information not inform, much of what is called knowledge management isn't. "You can't take knowledge and just give it to people. They have to *take* the knowledge," says Esther Dyson, cofounder of the Electronic Frontier Foundation.[1] Knowledge management hasn't earned its title until it starts improving the performance of content: Designing it so people want to take it and use it, and so they can ask better questions. Designing it in ways to quickly meet the needs of decision makers. Making it simpler to use, simpler to learn.

And This Is Good News?

You bet. If you could figure out the few places where changing the design of content would change people's questions and conversations, you could have an immediate impact on what they do to work smarter. Content design can have an immediate impact on the bottom line. Get clear and simple with content and you'll change how salespeople, customer reps, production crews, managers, and executives spend their time. This chapter will help you pick one or two places to get started.

On the next few pages there are eight stories about content design. They range from major breakthroughs and personal observations to what senior execs call "low-hanging fruit"—quick, easy wins. If you are wondering how they all come together, you can jump to the prototyping sidebar on page 151. There you will find the various disciplines of content design. For now, however, we'll focus on something smaller and more manageable. Search for the one nugget that creates a personal aha: There is so much to be done in content design—tackle *anything, anywhere*, and it's almost guaranteed that people will work smarter.

WHO'S LIKE ME?

Think back to Chapter 6 and the Behavioral Communication Model. The questions in that model help you focus on what people need to make decisions that can change their behaviors. Two of the questions are "How is this relevant to me?" and "How will I be measured?"

Gary Bosak and Sandy Kirmeyer at Sears worked backwards from these questions. Bosak, head of transformation, explains: "Sandy was a professor at Cornell University. Not only is she brilliant in understanding the power of information; she knows what makes our store managers tick."

"Many managers, like a lot of us, think their situation is unique. This can impede the sharing of best practices because the community they learn from is limited to a local district or geographic region. We needed to create connections between managers and find ways to increase sharing between all our stores."

"So Sandy helped us build the Sears Success Sharing System. It has four components: Review My Scores, Best Practices, Store Like Mine, and Action Planning. Our goal," Bosak continued, "was to make it easier for people to connect with each other, and for them to build upon what they had in common."

"For example: In Store Like Mine, a manager can search for the stores with the same sales volumes, number of employees, Sears credit card penetration; as well as how those stores scored in any of the sixteen measures of associate satisfaction—(like two-way communication, which has five different dimensions)—and just about any other dimension of running a store and managing people."

"Also the interface made it fun to discover these things. We designed it like a game. Suddenly, a manager in, let's say, Dallas, was discovering friends in Florida, New York, California, and all over. In Store Like Mine, the system gives you the top 10 matches of 33 different store and market characteristics. Because each characteristic has so many layers of detail, it's not uncommon for all ten to be very close matches."

"Then the measures did the rest. If there are 20 stores in the district, nobody wants to be number 20. And the top few want to proudly show what they did to get there. It's just common sense," concludes Bosak, "and organizing information in ways that foster connections between people. Not only has sharing increased tremendously in the areas where the system is in place, but I see a lot more of the ideas being implemented quickly."

DESIGN NOTES: Are the five topics within the Behavioral Communication Model built into your knowledge management system?

1. Relevance
2. Action

3. Measures and Consequences

4. Tool Descriptions

5. WIIFM

Are they woven directly into the content? Are they guiding your designs? If not, your system is wasting time and talent, because people may be sharing and learning, but they're not getting exactly what they need to change their behaviors.

GETTING STARTED: Ask your managers and front-line associates to participate in the design of collaborate spaces like the Sears Success Sharing System. Guide the design process using the Behavioral Communication Model discussed in Chapter 6.

EXPLAINING THINGS

Nigel Holmes explains the world in which we live. Like how much toothpaste Americans use every day. (If squeezed in a straight line, a daily dose takes you from Los Angeles to New York, with 50 miles left over.) Or how big is an IMAX screen? (5.5 taxicabs wide and 7 elephants high.)

Beginning in the late '70s, Holmes revolutionized how *Time* magazine visualized charts, diagrams, and graphics. He now has his own firm, Explanation Graphics.

What is one of his biggest challenges? "I've had work rejected because the explanations look too simple. I try to edit things down to the most critical elements and explain a process in ways that are easy to understand. But many clients still think more is more," says Holmes. "And they love their own jargon."

Hmmm: Would your associates work smarter if you instantly fired any consultant caught speaking jargonese?

DESIGN NOTES: Why do senior execs bring content designers in at the end of the planning process, to package their completed strategies? Why not bring in the content designers earlier in the process? Somewhere out there, you have a competitor rewriting this approach.

Thoughtful design of decision-making content should begin a lot earlier than many corporate planners believe. When people like Holmes are part of a strategic planning team, they can influence the way a strategy develops. Their input might even change the strategy itself. Because their priority is to create order through clarity instead of through mandate. Some New Economy firms have already figured out that one expert in explaining things can be worth more than a gaggle of senior vice planners.

GETTING STARTED: It's all about leadership. Senior execs need to evaluate their tolerance for inviting someone into the planning process whose role is to argue against mandate and replace it with clarity.

WHAT DESIGN CHANGED THE HISTORY OF PARIS?

Guess again. Think practical…think sewers. Thanks to the Seine, the Romans called Paris Lutetia: City of Mud. French novelist Victor Hugo devoted 15 pages in *Les Misérables*, to Paris' sewers. Why? More growth, more waste. And at one point, waste removal had as much impact as social, cultural, and political forces.

DESIGN NOTES: If a city were vying for your corporate headquarters, you wouldn't spend much time talking about sewers. They'd be a given, right? It's no different for knowledge systems. At some point, content becomes waste. So content design has to include waste removal.

Have you designed a sewer system? Is the process for getting rid of content as simple as flushing a corporate-wide e-toilet? Don't laugh. Go back to the dots on page 35. Without hassle-free procedures and tools, you are forcing knowledge workers to swim in their own waste. (Technology can do much of the work invisibly. But not until companies get as serious about information overload as they are about physical pollution.)

GETTING STARTED: Don't focus on technology. Focus on accountability. Who is in charge of your sewer system? While every associate has personal accountability for his or her own files, huge amounts of waste are clogging team and corporate-owned pipelines.

In the future, IT strategies may have as much accountability for waste removal as for creating new capacity. HR, Training, or Organizational Effectiveness will be looking at how people capacity is reduced by all the waste floating around. They will take the role of knowledge-worker advocate. And senior execs may be evaluated on their efforts to clean up knowledge work pollution in the same ways that manufacturing execs are now held accountable for physical pollution.

WHEN CONTENT DRIVES DIALOGUE

Root Learning has taken two simple disciplines and married them into a powerful business tool. The Perrysburg, Ohio, firm creates Learning Maps, which fuse strategy with learning.

Randy Root, founder, describes what they do. "First, we have found that visualizing strategies accelerates learning. It's easy to remember the big picture when it is literally a picture. To create that visual, we spend hundreds of hours pouring over client data, selecting, editing, and focusing it until a story emerges. All that work helps people see a huge, complicated story in the shortest possible time."

"Before going live, we test our designs. We watch and listen to the discussion the map creates," Root continues. "It's important to study how people use the information within the map. We then adjust the metaphors, visuals, questions, and instructions."

"The second, and more important, discipline is using the visuals to create dialogue. Specifically, Socratic dialogue. We avoid presenting senior management's conclusions. Instead, the map is set up for table discussions, and the employees discover their own answers. Effective dialogue should minimize how much leaders have to say and maximize what comes out of a learner's search," says Root. "It sounds simple, but it wouldn't work without content that has been specifically designed to move the conversation forward, and encourage people to come to their own conclusions."[2]

Jim Haudan, Root Learning's president, adds a critical point: "Once you've been through the process, you realize it's really a leadership tool. In order to create the maps, we first engage leaders in creating a story that can be visualized." (See Chapter 8 for more on storytelling.) **DESIGN NOTES:** I count Haudan and Root as friends and believe they are peerless in what they do. But simplicity demands that they and we change.

In most companies, tools like Learning Maps accelerate learning, yet little of their content is carried into day-to-day execution. Any firm wishing to get simple must recognize that learning and work can no longer be separated. Strategy rollout, learning, and the information we use every day need to be designed as one integrated whole. Richard Saul Wurman calls this "technotainment"—tools and technology that merge work information, entertainment, and learning opportunities.

Here is one way that might play out: One of your customer service reps—Sue—attends a meeting to learn about the new corporate strategy, designed to increase customer satisfaction. Because the strategy is visualized and the story and dialogue are so powerful, Sue has many new aha's. As the meeting ends, she learns that the company has changed her daily worktools to incorporate much of what she has just learned.

When Sue returns to her PC, she discovers that the new interface reflects the materials she just experienced. When she navigates through internal information, she finds that the visuals, language, and information hierarchies were designed in tandem with her face-to-face learning experience. Everything reinforces the strategy of improving customer satisfaction.

Sue's online customer satisfaction tool has also changed. A small fuel gauge has been added. As her customer scores go up or down, the gauge shows progress toward her bonus or toward the department's goals. When she clicks on the gauge, she rediscovers the connections between her department's performance and the strategy, because several visuals from the strategy rollout are hyperlinked to her fuel gauge. (With detailed text documents one more click away.)

Suddenly, the conversation between your rep and her manager changes. Because the connections between her scores and corporate strategies have been built into the customer service tool, their daily dialogue begins to build upon those connections. When Sue checked her customer satisfaction scores, she also clicked on the hyperlinked line: "Last quarter's top performing associate, John Doe, tells what he did to drive customer satisfaction through the roof. Click and go for more details." As a result, she starts bringing ideas from another business unit into team meetings.

Like all of us, Sue learns a lot from her teammates during her coffee breaks. After one break, she went back to her tool to see what everybody was talking about. She clicked on the hyperlinked line "Take the 'Tick Off the Customer' Quiz: The 10 worst customer complaints from last quarter, and what to do to avoid them."

GETTING STARTED: The technology for this scenario—dynamically generated information, hyperlinks, etc. —has existed for years. That is not the challenge. What is needed is the corporate willingness to work backwards from the content the workforce needs for decision making, and to link worktools, learning, and strategies together.

Content designers study what people talk about when they do their work. Is anyone in your company charged with studying the conversations your worktools create? You could learn so much about simplicity if you just listened to, and designed from, those conversations.

WHEN WAS THE LAST TIME A DAILY TRANSACTION EXCITED YOU?

Peter Moore is a partner at Inferential Focus, an intelligence-gathering firm based in New York City. He and his three partners have built a unique practice. They are hired to watch connections, patterns, and trends that most of us miss.

Moore has strong opinions on what it takes to ensure that information informs. "I think knowledge management is going down the wrong path," he says. "Codifying, collecting, and making everything accessible is less important than how it's used. Or how it's read. Organizations need to spend a lot more time thinking about the context of information: How you juxtapose one fact against another…how you debate what they mean…how you study or create the connections between ideas."

"Most of knowledge management is doing a great disservice to innovation, creativity, and spontaneity. Somebody at a conference said to me that it's all about the person with the chocolate bumping into the person with the peanut butter," Moore says with a smile. "I'd only add that it's important for both of them to understand what they have and what could happen if they put the two things together."

DESIGN NOTES: Moore and his partners are big on context. So are most companies. Yet business always complicates the process of bringing context into daily decisions. Most firms operate on the belief that there's work, and then there's time set aside for context setting. We don't have time for the two to be separate. Context has to be built into day-to-day transactions.

For example, go back to the customer satisfaction tool in the previous story. The context for making decisions wasn't limited to an offsite meeting or learning event; it was in the tool itself.

GETTING STARTED: Focus on accountability for building context into transactions. Do you have a Peanut Butter and Chocolate Team, responsible for removing the artificial boundaries between work, learning, and attention?

The companies that get simpler faster will use teams to answer questions like these: Does our performance management tool get people excited and thirsty for more? Is it a blast to discover what our other divisions are doing? Could we use customer satisfaction reports as recruitment tools? Do our strategy presentations motivate people to do extra research on their own? And: How long would it take a new hire to figure out our corporate strategy just by using our tools?

If you're not comfortable responding to these questions, get comfortable. Fast. Everything you build, including what's inside worktools, must compete in the Attention Economy (see Chapter 4). Simpler companies understand that content for decision making must hold its own against CNN, MTV, Amazon.com, Disney World, and the Discovery Channel.

FOOD FOR THOUGHT FOR LARGE, GLOBAL FIRMS

If you've got tens of thousands of employees all over the globe, waiting for people and ideas to bump into each other isn't very efficient. Grey Warner explains that sometimes it's better to let computers make many of the connections, then ask people to do the creative part. Warner is the head of Latin America Human Health for Merck.

"MIRRIAM is a computer-assisted business planning process developed by Merck" says Warner. "It allows us to have a consistent

PROTOTYPING CONTENT FOR DECISION MAKING

Content is power. All associates know this. But Net Geners will focus on content to push the boundaries of what is now called empowerment. Because as long as the company controls the three disciplines of content design, lots of what is needed to make decisions is in the hands of people who are far removed from those decisions. Will you lead your organization into the right-hand column? Or wait to be pushed there by Net Geners?

CONTENT DISCIPLINE	DEFINITION	WHAT WILL CHANGE
Information Architecture	Provides the framework and hierarchy for organizing ideas. (For example, corporate strategy and e-space design)	• Representatives of the entire associate population, not just IT and senior management, will be included in the design of the framework for ideas • Information measures on navigation, fulfillment, and time will become as common as customer and performance measures
Information Design	Provides the context: Builds relationships between ideas and the way they are expressed	• Representatives of the entire associate population, not just IT and senior management, will be included in design teams • Teams will get disciplined about context. Wherever it adds value, they will package context for the worktool design teams. (For example, see redesigned customer satisfaction tool described on page 148.)
Worktool Design	Provides the information people need to make daily work decisions	• IT and senior management will cede content design to the people making day-to-day decisions. (For example, customer service reps will design the customer reports they need, as well as how and when they will be used.)

process for resource allocation throughout the Latin America Region.

"First, it asks for data—like the sales response of our products to promotion—to enable us to decide how the different countries in the region get resourced. In some areas of the world, like the United States, lots of good data are readily available. In many of the countries I manage, the information is just not there. So MIRRIAM provides consistent ways to make the best possible estimates. This is critical because without good data, it's essential to have the right kind of debate, to get the best possible judgment from the organization given the information available. That's what MIRRIAM is really about, valuable conversation."

"Second, by virtue of how the data are organized, MIRRIAM makes it easier for different functions to get together. Sales, marketing, finance and all the others have a common view, a common language," states Warner.

"Finally, MIRRIAM has greatly enhanced how many scenarios we can consider. In a few hours, people can produce 50 alternative business plans. So we use the power of the computer to do multiple analyses on different factors like sales response at different levels of resources."

And why is this approach to resource allocation important? "The beauty of it is that, market by market, you're looking at plans that are developed and reviewed in a consistent manner," says Warner. "That lets us get to the important and creative parts of the conversation quickly. Where do we make trade-offs? Will we get greater return on the same effort in Brazil or Colombia? It's all about consistency of analysis to get to the part that a computer can't do—using judgment, making the decisions that make a difference," says Warner.

What's not to love? "At first there was a lot of resistance to this approach, usually, because people were concerned about added work, and what the process might reveal."

"If the content for our discussions is developed in a consistent manner, the trends—good and bad—are easier to spot. This meant we had to create an environment where people feel they are safe to be open and transparent. The centerpiece of all this has nothing to do with data-crunching or analysis. We had to do a lot of work to create a culture

PROTOTYPING THE FUTURE

Want to study the future of content design? Don't look to Corporate America. Most companies are still in the dark ages.

Read *Rolling Stone.* There you can watch the unfolding struggle between content providers (recording labels) and New Economy listeners. Armed with technology like MP3, Liquid Audio, and a2b, kids in high school are downloading content (music) from the Net for free. Major labels are rethinking strategies to ensure that they are not cut out of the loop. And everyone involved is trying to figure out new methods of payment.

If you think it's laughable that huge chunks of your infrastructure—information architecture, information design, and worktool design—will be ceded to the workforce, talk to recording industry execs. They will ask: Do you think the kids who are bypassing the providers and downloading Limp Bizkit or *Soundbombing II* will suddenly do an about-face because they believe that your kind of content is different? That they should let you control the content and infrastructure they need to work smarter?

"The issue is about clarification.

The idea is to go for the interrelationships between the information we use to make decisions."

LEIF EDVINSSON, Director of Intellectual Capital, Skandia

where both good and bad news could be handled completely out in the open."

"In some countries, it took several years before we were ready to use tools like MIRRIAM. My most important job was to make sure Merck's values and business principles—trust, integrity, transparency (meaning the whole truth), and others—were the foundation for our discussions," concludes Warner.

DESIGN NOTES: Top-performing companies, like Merck, are extremely sophisticated in developing the content for strategic planning discussions. Their executives, like Grey Warner, also work hard to create environments where individuals can thrive. Yet how many large firms are bringing global sophistication down to personal worktools? (Merck has begun. See Wendy Dixon's and John Yates' stories on pages 56 and 113.)

Big companies have to work harder than everyone else to design content for decision making:

- The New Economy is rewarding a lot of the best talent for starting their own business or working for smaller firms. If you want to attract that talent, you have to be better at building what they need to work smarter, faster.
- By definition, larger companies are harder to navigate, and they create more noise than smaller companies.
- The workforce will evaluate whether they can trust you to help them work smart enough, fast enough. Among their criteria are easy navigation and less noise.

If you are a large, global company, associates will demand and expect "MIRRIAM-like" sophistication in many of their workaday tools. For the kids who grew up on the Net, it will not seem unreasonable to expect content to do as much work in community yellow pages or customer reports as it does inside the tools reserved for the executive suite and R&D.

GETTING STARTED: The challenge is not technology. At its current rate of change, MIRRIAM-like sophistication will soon be available for most corporate tools. The question is: Are large companies willing to design content and tools for business units of one—the individual? Because this is where smaller, New Economy firms will kick butt.

WHO IS DESIGNING YOUR CONTENT FOR E-SPACES: SOMEONE SKILLED IN THINKING ABOUT THINKING?

A lot of work gets done in your e-spaces—from intranets and teleconferences, and everything in between—but who is designing these spaces and what goes inside them? Are your techno-wonks also skilled in helping people think? Don Winkler provides a good reason why you might want to expand the list of people who contribute to how these spaces are designed.

Winkler is chairman and CEO of Ford Motor Credit Company, the world's largest automotive finance company. He has spent his entire life living with dyslexia.

"I go to bed at nine and wake up at three, for two reasons," he says. "Mostly, it's because I have so much fun doing what I do. I have a very strong sense of purpose. I also get up early because I need to prepare differently than many people. My laptop, the Internet, clipping services—everything needs to be cross-tabbed. And if it wasn't for my Palm Pilot, I'd never know where to be when."

What can dyslexia and other learning differences, which affect 15 percent of our population, teach us about content? "I see dyslexia as a gift," Winkler says. "It has taught me a lot about organizing information. Before I had all the technology I do now, I had to develop coping mechanisms. I learned to organize information just enough to ask the questions that got me to the real issues. I couldn't afford for meetings and conversations to produce even more for me to sift through. Most information just produces more complexity."

"I later learned that my ways of coping were teaching me to think about thinking. I realized that the real point of most information is to bring the conversation to a higher level. To help people ask better questions. And to create breakthroughs."

"For example," Winkler continued, "a few years ago, the bank I worked for was wrestling with some very complicated issues in our industry. My team and I spent a lot of time organizing information so people would focus on the contradictions, gaps, and opportunities. So more people would ask different kinds of questions."

"During a breakthrough meeting, Yolanda, a clerk in one of our branches, asked a very simple, yet powerful, question. She asked: 'Our goal is to do whatever it takes to serve every person that comes into the bank, right? Yet you just said only 50 out of every 100 people get their loan applications approved. Where do the other 50 go?' "

"The answer," says Winkler, "was that these loan turndowns were walking out the door and going to finance companies, which provide loans to people with less-than-perfect credit. So Yolanda asked a second question: 'Don't we have a finance company at our bank?' The answer was yes."

"Yolanda's questions led to a major breakthrough. We created a referral program that now accounts for over $150 million a month in new loan volume. All because Yolanda asked, and someone listened."

Winkler concludes: "To me, that's what simplicity in information design is all about: Designing the information in ways so people ask new and tougher questions and have better conversations."

DESIGN NOTES: Winkler is often called upon within his organization to guide the discussions that create breakthroughs. You have the opportunity to do the same thing—and go further.

You could be asking teammates skilled in "thinking about thinking" to move beyond facilitation. They could be designing your e-spaces. Do you have people with organizational effectiveness, anthropology, sociology, or change agent backgrounds contributing to how content is organized, visualized, and compared? Are they the ones studying and listening to your associates as they use your tools?

Or is that left to the techno-wonks? If so, your associates are probably working too hard to see the connections and contradictions buried within your e-spaces.

GETTING STARTED: Again, focus on accountability. Whose bonus is based on making content, not just technology, easy to use?

DESIGN: HOW TO THRIVE ON AMBIGUITY

Fresh out of the University of Chicago, Matt Percy joined Monsanto in the Nutrition and Consumer Products Sector. "I do whatever's needed, but I guess my title is Assistant to the President and Content Developer. Right now I'm researching soy and health food products. I go back and forth between doing market research and talking to store clerks," says Percy. "I'm also part of the Web development team, and I work as a liaison between the marketing group and the product development group to facilitate communication."

"I'm glad he gave himself that title," says Percy's boss, Nick Rosa. "Matt is a good example of how we're trying to break the mold on the challenges we all face. Everyone is in decision overload. I can't say Monsanto is the ultimate success story, but we're working on it. People's jobs are getting so complex, we need to find new ways to address that kind of overload."

"Matt is part of a growing number of people we hire to help with content development. They attend senior-level meetings. They are part of strategic planning. They go out to different regions of the world and observe. They make sure the senior team doesn't get caught up in its own shorts," jokes Rosa. "We're trying to take some of the roles usually reserved for consultants and give them to people like Matt."

Nick Rosa feels the overload of complexity firsthand. He recently was promoted from division president to corporate senior vice president at Monsanto. His new duties include development of a global leadership team and acceptance of biotechnology around the world.

"We're building a place that is different from most," says Rosa. "We're throwing a lot of ambiguity and shared responsibility at people. We have what we call 'two in the box.' For some senior positions, we've determined that two separate disciplines are really important. Like commercial development and research. So we don't pick one person to be the head of a department. We have coleaders. That's not appealing to some people. We get push-back: 'You mean I'm not in charge? I thought my title was going to be such-and-such.' My response is, 'I don't care if you call yourself the Grand Poobah. Titles are occasionally useful in the outside world. But internally, the position is too complex for one person.'"

"We're creating an environment where people will self-select into or out of their roles. For them to work through that much ambiguity," concludes Rosa, "they need content that is designed and customized for the way they make decisions."

DESIGN NOTES: Everybody wants his or her role to be clear. Yet we're moving in a direction where there will be more ambiguity, and people will have to create their own role clarity. Much of the accountability for creating that clarity rests with the individual. But not all. Companies are responsible for worktool content and making it simple to use. **GETTING STARTED:** When the right tools and environment are provided, ambiguity can be a good thing. It can spur people on to new levels of creativity and innovation. Have you thought about doubling, even tripling, the amount of ambiguity you throw at people? It can be done. If, like Matt Percy and Nick Rosa, you are constantly working backwards from the content people need to make decisions in an ambiguous world. To get started, ask those people for an in-depth description of the top five tools they would use—and exactly how they would work—if you cut their role clarity in half. After some kicking and screaming, you will get valuable insights.

Simpler for Whom?

Details, details, details. The devil of content design is in the details. It's the hard work behind empowered decision making.

No company claims to have mastered making content simpler to use. Off the record, some will admit that design excellence may complicate executive responsibilities. For example, reread the Store Like Mine story (on page 144). Tons of measures had to be tracked, statistically validated, organized, and linked so that one manager could find common ground with another.

So why would anyone build a simpler company by focusing on content design? It comes down to an organization's capacity for learning, which can create competitive advantages. Being user centered in content design changes the performance of information. People can get a lot more out of less—not through some management or consultant's flavor of the month, but because the raw materials for decision making were designed for how people learn, and, equally important, how they talk to one another.

It has been said that process design includes watching what people do to simplify tasks, then building the "work-arounds" into the process. Content design is no different. If your designs are based on what interests people, and how they want to talk to each other, you will find that leaders can say a lot less. And people's curiosity will do a lot more of the work.

Content Design: In One Word

Elegance.

Ignite your associates' imagination with the elegance of your worktools. No matter what you do to earn profits, you are also a content provider to knowledge workers. And in the Attention Economy, the return on elegance is faster, smarter work.

"Even if we're working in an organization of experts, 90 percent of the time we're in situations where we're not the expert. We need to rely on content design that helps us get what we need in the shortest time. Anything that prevents that from happening is going to render this whole approach useless."

PEHONG CHEN
President, BroadVision

"Our Technology Transfer Group is really a content translation service. They are a group of scientists whose charge in life is to take R&D technical information and translate it for marketing and sales needs."

HILDRA TROTTER
Knowledge Process Leader, Dow AgroSciences

Chapter **12**

Simpler to Do

Using project design to make informed choices

The strongest principle of growth lies in human choice.

Mary Ann Evans, whose books celebrate simple folks in complicated situations

When I was four or five, one of my favorite toys was Mr. Machine. He was a see-through mechanical man, designed to expose the inner workings of gears and pulleys that made him go. The hours I spent studying him inspired me (much to Mom's dismay) to graduate to toasters, a sewing machine, and a brand new television.

Would you like a Mr. Machine for simplicity? A window to watch how it all comes together and a place to examine its inner workings? That place would be the early stages of project design.

Moving from Tasks to Choices

If you go to this window but ask the wrong questions, you could miss the simpler moment. To catch it, you need to ask, "Why do we have projects? Why not move straight from the corporate plan into work?"

If your firm is like most, project design is about producing a "to do" list that can be tracked and managed. It is the place where strategies, goals, and ideas get chunked down, then divvied into specific tasks and activities. And where personal accountabilities get assigned.

Simpler companies think differently. They understand that projects are also the exact place and time where corporate, personal, team, and customer needs converge on a manageable scale. For a brief moment— during the first few team meetings when a project is being designed— all the trade-offs and choices that everyone must make get debated and discussed.

At simpler companies, the view through the window during these early design sessions is a snapshot of all the choices people will face

CHAPTER PUNCHLINE

Simpler companies feed the fire of personal choice.
They sponsor a healthy debate between
opting out and buying in.

**PROJECT LEADERS
TO EXECS**

"Dontcha get it?

Every day
we discuss what
others need
to make choices."

**THE MODEL
FOR SIMPLER
TO DO**

Go to the one place
where you could learn the
most about the choices
people face: Project
design meetings.

Study hard.
Push what you learn—
especially the ideas that
upset the status quo—
into the fabric of the
organization.

THE MODEL IN ACTION

As you've seen throughout
this section, the model is
often put into practice for
customers. All customer
driven organizations do at
least one thing very well:
They are aggressive in
driving customer needs
throughout the
organization. They "force"
rapid change, not by
mandate, but by letting the
voice of the customer serve
as a wake-up call and
rallying cry.

**WHY MANY COMPANIES
DON'T FOLLOW THE
MODEL**

Apparently, they must
believe complexity ain't so
bad. Because very few
companies aggressively
drive associate needs and
questions throughout the
organization. As a matter of
fact, many do their best to
bury the debate that raises
these issues.

once the project "goes live." For example:

- Choices that the project team will make: "Given all our other accountabilities, how much do we really want to invest in this project? Are we convinced that it's worth it?"
- Choices that leadership will make: "For this project to succeed, the senior team is going to have to change how they lead. Have they signed up for that?"
- Choices that associates will make: "Will the people who have to implement this buy in to all the changes? Will they be excited? Pissed? Or just on overload?"
- Choices that customers will make: "What about this project would convince customers to leave the competition?"
- Choices that vendors will make: "Why would they agree with how we want to change our inventory controls?"

Project design is really about organizing choices. If you are looking for it, you can see the exact moment where multi-audience, complex, and interconnected choices become clear.

Yet most companies ignore this moment, focusing instead on the "to do" list that comes out of the discussion.

"Opening up boundaries is about how our thinking shapes our behavior. Leaders need to be much more aware of the environment—which includes the choices people are facing."

RON SCHULTZ, Santa Fe Center for Emergent Strategies; author, *Open Boundaries*

PROJECT TEAMS

Supply the issues, questions, concerns, and ideas that could help others make choices

SENIOR EXECS

Sponsor the debate

THE DEBATE

is what creates clarity for implementation issues like, "What do I do when everything is an 'A' priority?" That kind of clarity doesn't come from plans, checklists, or even shared mindset.

The importance of thinking differently as you look through the project design window *cannot be overemphasized*. Even in the best-managed organizations, the choices people have to make come loaded with conflicting priorities, paradoxes, and necessary compromises. For the average associate, the toughest part of getting his or her work done is making sense of all the conflicts.

Simpler companies respond by tapping into everything that project leaders and their teams know that might help. In addition to all the sanctioned stuff—like databases filled with "best practices"—they ask project leaders for the questions and concerns that usually go unrecorded. They look for the things that don't make it into official "aren't we happy" documents that are written to guide major changes.

What Happens Next Is Counterintuitive for Most Senior Execs

Simpler companies not only make it possible, they make it hard to avoid ideas that upset the status quo. Open discussion and debate is key to what makes simpler companies different and makes them work better.

The leaders of these firms push debates about the choices everyone is facing into the fabric of the organization. That means that simpler companies do things like:

- Posting guides comparing the pros *and cons* of buying into the next big change on the company intranet. No hype. The material is written as if *Consumer Reports* had done the research.
- Creating more balance in major events, for example, by mixing point/counterpoint meetings with rallies and celebrations.
- Using the intranet to publicize the ways that associates have found to bypass the officially sanctioned tools and processes in order to simplify their work. (Healthy competition is always a good thing. Maybe that posting will convince the next process redesign team to be more user centered.)
- Creating a culture where the most valued sources of information—electronic and personal—provide balanced views of the choices to be made during change.
- Sponsoring an "are we asking the right questions?" day, one month before the senior team plans to announce a new strategy. (Healthy competition applies to senior execs too. Can any leader say that the executive suite asks better questions than the rest of us?)

To many leaders, these are counterintuitive notions: "They look like distractions to me. Don't these things make more noise, competing with the one voice, shared mindset we are trying to create?"

According to the old rules, yes. According to the basic tenets of the Attention Economy, just the opposite. In a world filled with infinite choices, these debates are exactly what people need to make sense of all the conflicts and ambiguity.

For example: How do associates figure out what to do when there are 37 "A" priorities that were due yesterday and resources are stretched thin before they get past the first five? In the real world, there are few "B" priorities. Still we keep pretending that shared mindset and clear goals can make sense of this type of complexity. Discussions about choices help associates cut through the corporate spin and find out what is *really* important.

> **Again** (from Chapter 9): *Creating shared mindset and clear goals will always be critical, but do not confuse this work with simplicity. Simpler companies go one step further. They become user centered.*

And the only way to be user centered is to push the debate about choices into the open. A lot of companies do the opposite. They do their best to bury it.

A Case Study in Burying the Debate

Not long ago I was talking with a friend whom I deeply respect. He was wrestling with a tough assignment—managing a successful transition after the merger of two large companies.

Thinking I might be helping to make the complex clear, I listed some of the choices that over 100,000 people would face during the transition. Apparently, I misjudged what my friend expected from our conversation. Because it ended abruptly when he said, "You don't understand. There is only one choice."

He was right, of course. In the spirit of the flight controller who brought the crew of *Apollo 13* safely home, he meant "Failure is not an option."

And he was wrong. Because he also meant "The only choice on my radar screen, and the only choice that I will communicate, is the 'party line.'"

Unfortunately, not only is his firm not learning from the debate about choices that is happening among associates, but one of the people in charge of the transition feels that open discussion of those choices would be a distraction.

Although my friend's company is a powerhouse and well respected on Wall Street, confidential discussions among senior management are another matter. One of their biggest concerns is the complexity of all the work facing leaders and associates. Even some of our most admired companies find it hard to get simple by opening up the debate.

The Simpler Moment: A Technicolor Explosion

That brings us back to that simpler moment when we were looking through the project design window. Unleash a different kind of debate and you'll see a technicolor explosion of ideas that will make it possible for people to connect in completely new ways. You will get simpler implementation "for free."

All the work you put into content design will begin to pay off. Partially because the information is more useful. But mostly because people will look at it differently. Conversations about choices we must make change how we pay attention to the details in all our tools, emails, meetings, etc.

And it's not just the details. It's the passion and energy. Since most people want to make a difference, when you create a dialogue that makes personal (not just corporate) choices clear, people can choose to channel their passions into the things that make a difference. As a result, teamwork and community ties will be strengthened.

And it's not just passion. It's respect. Front-line associates have to juggle hundreds of conflicting priorities every day. Sponsoring the debate between opting out and buying in to these priorities says two things:

- Your company respects people as thinking adults. They should have whatever is available to make decisions, even if it conflicts with the party line.
- You are concerned about how the company uses people's time, and you are focused on using it more effectively and respectfully.

And it's not just respect. It is doing more to earn people's trust. Go back to Chapter 10: Net Geners will expand how we now think about trust. While previous generations *appreciate* more open debates about

continued on page 168

PROTOTYPING THE MOTHER OF ALL PROJECTS

You are riding in a submarine on tracks, just below the water's surface. Air bubbles and fish gurgle by. *Kerrr-chunk*: You dock at a schoolhouse. Inside, you discover lots of icons. Slowly, after several clues, you figure out that the icons are numbers, and that they will help you complete your mission.

This is how my then-11-year-old son, a Net Gener, described his favorite part of *Riven*, a simulation game. He still talks excitedly about learning how to make choices, how to piece together information he needed, and how those lessons applied to school assignments.

Simulation technology isn't just for kids. More and more, the tool helps businesses to examine the choices made by customers and competitors.

But why isn't it in widespread use for the mother of all projects—the annual budget? Why aren't all plant managers and business unit heads getting *Riven*-style simulations and told to "go play"? Simulation tools could not only help them come up with a budget; they could blur the boundary between learning and planning. Since the choices built into the budget can be extremely difficult and complex—**moving in this direction would seem to be a no-brainer.**

The challenge is not the cost or availability of technology. Mass-market simulations can be adapted; one gaming firm set up a business products division almost a decade ago. So why are the tools of budgeting more about control than learning how to make choices?

Because that's the point. Imagine the risks involved if a business gave *Riven*-style simulations to people doing budgets. The senior team might get back unexpected solutions. Innovation, creativity, and new ways of thinking would worm their way into a very controlled, orderly process. **We can't have that now, can we?**

"Net Geners are saying, 'All bets are off. If you want to *join us* in a discussion and contribute to how we decide, fine. But don't expect us to follow the corporate agenda without what we need.' Leaders will face two choices: Get people who are less motivated, or change the way the company responds to their needs."

PETER MOORE, Partner Inferential Focus

"Some of my social scientist friends say we're leaving lots of people out of the social contract and we will have a revolution. Maybe that's an overstatement. But clearly, we've got to rethink how we design work, controls, and how people make choices."

JIM CHAMPY, author, *Reengineering Management* and *The Arc of Ambition*

continued from page 165

buying in or opting out, Net Geners will *expect* that type of clarity.
Or they will automatically say good-bye.

Simpler companies understand all this and more. They do the
counterintuitive: They actively seek out the details and truths that only
come from the people at the heart of the organization. Having collected
all needs, concerns, choices, and perceptions, they sponsor the debate
to sort through it all.

Making Sure Your Project Leaders Are Ready

Much of this chapter has focused on what senior execs have to change.
To be fair, some project leaders and their teams will also have to adjust.
Not all have the skills, experience, or desire to recognize or pay
attention to all the trade-offs and choices discussed in the course of
project design.

Any firm that plans to move project leaders into this role should
make one article required reading. In the May 1999 issue of *Fast
Company*, Tom Peters wrote the ultimate guide. Among Peters' project
principles are:

- Never accept a project as given
- No project worth talking about happens without passion
- Project management is emotion management; it's about creating
  pulse-racing, mind-expanding possibilities
- Every project is an opportunity to take a new look at things
- No project is too small or mundane to become a "Wow" project
- "Wow" project leaders have two essential skills: Pitching and
  community organizing
- Project execution is about rapid prototyping; a series of
  approximations and instant feedback

In just a few pages, Peters sets the standard for project leadership.
Mix in most of Section 2 from this book, and you've got a self-
directed tutorial.

The Three Most Important Takeaways from This Chapter

First, conversation is what makes things simpler to do—not checklists
or any other management tool. Simpler execution is about having the
kind of conversations that help people make personal (not just
corporate) choices.

Second, let's not kid ourselves. Just because the amount of yacking inside your company has increased dramatically does not guarantee that people are getting what they need. As our study found, most communication and dialogue is not designed for today's fast-paced decision-making environment (see Chapter 2).

Finally: To get simple, business must accept a paradox: When you promote *only* the party line, you actually *decrease* people's ability to work smarter. In a world filled with infinite choices, the officially sanctioned window offers a very narrow view of what they need to make informed decisions. If you want to get simple, doing the counterintuitive is not up for debate. What we're talking about is how best to achieve clarity of personal choices.

SIMPLE NOTES

1. Bringing ideas that upset the status quo into the open in no way diminishes the value of rallying everyone behind a common goal and shared vision. It's the same as we've been telling our associates about living with paradoxes: "You've got to do that work *and* this work."

2. I may have used the terms *project design* or *project leader* differently than you do in your company. Feel free to substitute any term/title for the work that sits at the crossroads between strategy rollout and full-blown implementation. The key is to focus on the exact place where corporate, personal, team, and customer needs come together at a manageable scale. *Before* moving into implementation.

GETTING STARTED

Please DO NOT turn this into a knowledge management exercise in which codifying and collecting what project teams know becomes more important than the dialogue. Instead

1. Chat with a few project leaders

2. Sponsor the debate...fast!

3. Repeat steps 1 and 2, ad nauseam

Associates will quickly tell you which debates worked and which didn't.

USING PROJECT DESIGN TO ORGANIZE CHOICES

What would happen if companies worked backwards from the place where corporate, personal, team, and customer needs converge on a manageable scale? What would change if senior execs sponsored debates using what they learned from project leaders?

Here is a sampling of what that shift might look like. Not everything in the right-hand column should be implemented as described. The discussions set in motion by this table will help you figure out how much, or little, to change.

Experts on creativity and innovation call for pushing ideas that upset the status quo into the fabric of the organization. For example, Stan Gryskiewicz, a senior fellow at the Center for Creative Leadership, has asked senior execs to be more aggressive in creating "positive turbulence."

Simpler companies add a new dimension. They are user centered. The voices *in the middle of the organization* should create positive turbulence on leadership, governance, and performance structures. Ideally, no leader should have to sponsor this helpful tension. If true two-way dialogue existed, the changes in the right-hand column would just happen. On their own.

Now let's wake up and smell the coffee. In many (but not all) firms, user-centered ideas will not break into top-down structures without senior sponsorship.

DISCIPLINE OR FUNCTION	FROM CENTERED ON CHOICES THE COMPANY HAS MADE	TO CENTERED ON CHOICES INDIVIDUALS MUST MAKE
Leadership Development	**Senior execs talking to themselves** about the choices they face, and how they're doing.	**Project leaders create stretch goals for senior execs.** They know what it takes to do the work of customer focus and to implement the strategic plan.
Transformation/ Change	**"Don't look to us for details.** But do rally around the corporate flag."	Project team (using Chapters 4, 5 and 6): **"We can do a lot more** to help people make informed decisions."
Performance Management/ Governance	**"What controls and structures do we need?** What should we be measuring?"	**"What can we learn from the people who do the work?** 1. We've got too many measures in some areas and not enough in others. 2. We might want to rethink how we're about to restructure the company. The ideas from the front lines make more sense from the customer's point of view."
IT/Knowledge Management	**Creator and coordinator** of information access	IT/Knowledge Management assume **support roles.** Project leaders, who understand the needs of decision makers, assume lead roles.
Corporate Communication	"How can we help everyone understand and celebrate **the party line?"** The hierarchy for ideas comes from the top of the organization.	"How can we help everyone understand **the choices they are making?"** The hierarchy for ideas comes from project leaders. There's a creative tension between execs and the Communications Department.

Chapter 13

Simpler to Succeed

Designing work for easy navigation

No matter where you go, there you are.

Buckaroo Banzai, rock star, neurosurgeon, alien chaser

"Hello? I visited your museum almost 25 years ago, and, um…
Is anybody still around who can confirm my memories? There was
this maze with Ping-Pong balls and gates, and…"

This is how I first met Lesley Lewis, CEO of the Ontario Science
Centre, the place where this book began. After she answered my
questions, our conversation turned to the mission and innovations of
the museum. Lewis mentioned that the Centre was one of the earliest
museums, along with San Francisco's *Exploratorium*, to be dedicated
to making science both fun and highly interactive.

We discussed how NASA's *Challenger* disaster inspired the
Challenger Center for Space Science Education and the creation of
Challenger Learning Centers, one of which is at the Ontario Science
Centre. Simulations designed initially for use with school groups are
now also used to help corporate leaders learn about teamwork, role
clarity, and making tough, fast decisions in a world filled with
conflicting information and priorities.

It turns out that Lewis was facing some tough choices herself.
"When the Science Centre was first built," she said, "we provided few
signs or directions. We wanted everyone to create their own experience.
We even made it hard to walk in a straight line through the Centre.
The walkways, exhibits, and signage were designed to create a new
experience around every corner."

"Recently, we have realized that many of our visitors don't have the
time to use the Centre the way it was originally designed. Many parents

CHAPTER PUNCHLINE

It's a lot easier to succeed when the environment

is designed to help you get in;

get what you need; get out

succeed

WORKFORCE TO EXECS

"As consumers, we know this can be done!"

THE MODEL FOR SIMPLER SUCCESS

Make it easy for people to find their own way and they'll be more successful more often.

THE MODEL IN ACTION

(Again…) The model is everywhere you go as a *consumer.* Go to your favorite museum or get a map for a city you've never visited. Or pick up any well-designed directory. All follow two basic tenets:

- You are in control of your choices. Where you go and what you do is not mandated by some organization's strategic plan.
- The framework that guides you must be based on what you are trying to achieve, not what someone else wants you to achieve.

WHY THIS IS A LOW PRIORITY FOR MOST COMPANIES

(Again…) It's all about assumptions. Most companies say, "Here is our strategy and business plan. Now connect all your work to it." It is an extremely rare company that turns the whole thing around to be user centered: "Gee. What if we designed guides and maps and resource centers for whatever our associates are trying to achieve? If we've done our job well, our strategic plan and infrastructure will be transparent—there, but not in the way."

come in and only have an hour or two, but they still want their visit to be a great learning experience and exciting. We've responded with improved maps and different signage. But we need to do more."

"The paradox," Lewis concludes, "is that our mission—one of discovery and fun—is bumping up against the need for speed and ease of use. It comes down to navigation. To successfully compress discovery and learning, you have to be able to find your way around. It needs to be very easy for our visitors to come in, get what they want, probably get something additional they didn't expect, and leave happy and excited."

The Need to Change How We Design Work

Lewis' insights tee up a discipline that is critical if you want to create a simpler company—navigation.

It's great that most businesses are focused on reversing Industrial Age practices. (Stressing team solutions over command decisions, focusing on core processes, pushing decisions closer to the customer, etc.) All these efforts will surely help the *company* succeed. But they do little to meet a basic human need for success.

The more chaotic, new, volatile or interconnected any situation becomes, the more navigation—the discipline that helps us to pick and choose among choices—becomes a driving force. It is an undeniable human instinct to stop the music and say, "Hold on. Where am I? What's around me? How do I find what I need?"

Navigation provides tools (directional signs, guides, indexes, maps, warning signs, etc.) and frameworks to help people answer these questions and more. Companies use the principles of navigation to create relationships and paths between ideas. And now that a lot of information comes to us digitally, navigation also gives us the ability to control speed, zooms, scrolls, perspectives, and to create our own paths and relationships. When environments are on choice and information overload, awesome navigation isn't just a nice to-do. It's a necessity.

Personal success is no longer just about compensation, career development, work/life balance, etc. It's also about navigation: "Am I working in an environment that makes it easy to find my own way? Can I get in, get what I need, and get out?"

So What?

Unfortunately, many firms just don't get a major tenet of navigation—
that frameworks and guides must be based on what an individual is
trying to achieve, not what the company wants out of that work.

Said more bluntly: The company strategy or business plan ain't no
navigation tool.

For any navigation system to work, its designers must ask "What is
the user trying to achieve?" then work backwards from there. It's OK to
think of your strategy as providing the content that people need to do
their job. But don't go calling it a "change map," which tags it as a
how-to tool. Anything with that title needs to answer navigational
questions like: Who knows what I don't? Who's done this before? Is it
easy for me to assess how far I have to go and how much work there is
to be done? If not, where do I turn? etc.

Simpler companies will understand that these are the right questions
to be thinking about. And they'll start building new navigational tools
to help people find their own answers. They may design internal call
centers to help associates locate who or what they need to solve a
problem. Or they'll design "go to" reference points that are consistent
whether associates come across them on the intranet, in a training class,
or during the next strategy rollout. Or they may spend a lot more time
thinking about how their physical space, like conference rooms, help or
hurt people who are trying to work smarter.

The ways to create simpler navigation are limitless. However, there
are only a few things to consider when getting started, because they
involve changing how we think about navigation.

First, to make it simpler for individuals to succeed, some senior
execs may need to go through a mind-shift. The Strategy or The Plan
may help *executives* navigate change, but since these things are not user
centered, they rarely help the average associate in the same way.
Navigation has little to do with the structures you put in place to run
the business, like strategic plans, budgets, governance, or how business
units are organized.

Second, although information technology may be the vehicle of
choice, navigation is NOT about putting a few directional signals on all
your e-spaces. To design work for easy navigation, it is important to
look at your infrastructure the way your associates experience it. That

means you need to think about how people development, information development, and technology converge—viewing your company as one big integrated information space. (See "Thinking Bigger Than E-Spaces: A Lot Bigger," on page 181.)

Finally, let's go back to those pesky Net Geners. If easy navigation is not a priority at your firm, you may hear "I'm outta here" from many in this population. More loudly and defiantly than any generation before.

Add those things together and you get a new view of navigation: It's holistic. (Can I get what I need to work smarter anyplace, anytime, in any way?) And it's user centered. (Can I find my own way?)

How to Navigate This Chapter

On page 185, you'll find a framework for thinking about navigation in all areas of your company. To be candid, however, its view is from 30,000 feet. Think of the framework as helpful context.

For ideas that you can put to use, surf the next few pages. You'll find several stories and sidebars that range from information structures to the rooms we use, to the services that tomorrow's associates may come to expect. Search for the one or two ideas that get you started thinking about navigation in a different way. Then transfer your aha's into the template in Chapter 9, "A Strategy for Simpler, Smarter Work."

SMASHING THE BOUNDARY

Leif Edvinsson is corporate director of intellectual capital at Skandia AFS and is a leading expert on intellectual capital.

"To me," says Edvinsson, "what we're talking about is knowledge navigation. Every day brings new, unknown territories. You have to continually find out what you don't know. This can be really complex if everything is organized according to a top-down approach. The only way to figure this out is from the individual's perspective."

"My continuing work at Skandia has been to build and refine our Navigator. It's an online tool that picks up data about business growth from various databases and regroups it into a pedagogical format." [Kitchen-table translation: It's organized to make it easy to see the connections between each trend.]

"If you click on the Navigator, you see real-time changes in Skandia's intellectual capital, which includes measures on financials, customers, processes, people, continuous improvement and innovation."

"Just as important, however, is that every individual at Skandia can develop a personal Navigator. The goal is for everyone to understand how they are creating value for themselves, the company, and for our customers. It's not that complicated. A template helps you to visualize your mission, critical success factors, and strategic indicators. Of course," concludes Edvinsson, "your personal Navigator is for you alone. It's never publicly available."

DESIGN NOTES: Skandia's Navigator creates customized, personal views of performance information. They are breaking down the boundary that most companies maintain between performance and collaborative information. In most firms, it's still difficult for associates to customize and cross-reference trends between all the data within corporate performance systems.

This boundary affects how lots of companies approach "open-book management" or the balanced scorecard—slightly more traditional variations on Skandia's Navigator. These companies often say things like "We are educating our people about key performance indicators." And the sharing of industry trends, sales, and profitability with associates is called "employee education" or "communication."

How paternalistic. It's the associates' data. They did the work that generated it. They need it to do their job. Easy navigation begins when you smash the boundary between performance and collaborative systems. This would eliminate the need for a whole lot of "education."

GETTING STARTED: In tech-talk, smashing the boundary is called *transparency*. With this new access it should be just as easy for an associate to, for example,

- Grab some customer data,
- Overlay it with this quarter's goals, and
- Then compare the mix with her personal performance report…

…as it is for her to log onto the intranet in search of customer-focused best practice.

But the place to start, is not by focusing on tools or technology. Instead, senior execs need to talk to each other. They need to take a position on how little or how much transparency they want designed

continued on page 180

NAVIGATION: THE BEST-KEPT SECRET, HIDDEN IN PLAIN SIGHT

Much of your future is being invented now at the MIT Media Lab. In the early 1990s, Muriel Cooper led one of MIT's teams in creating Information Landscapes, an awesome approach to navigating anything you want to know. Yet, for the most part, **the idea sits there, languishing.** Hardly any firms have explored its potential.

The New York Stock Exchange has. Their virtual trading floor allows traders to fly through noise and zoom in on specific activities and data sets, color-coded and layered with the exact indicators they need. Idealab!, a firm that jump-starts new Internet companies, has taken this idea even further.

In Idealab!'s system, the user flies through pictures. So instead of dealing with filenames of, let's say, art history, you zoom past a Warhol and Mona Lisa, back in time to a Grecian sculpture.

Imagine a space where associates can zoom through your strategic plan (pictures of your products and services) into a 3-D space that shows their projects.

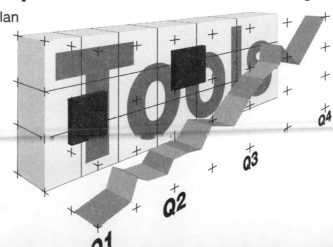

Then behind the projects are layers of toolkits: Best Practices, Coaching, Communicating, whatever. The toolkits become immersive experiences, way beyond checklist tutorials. Fly to the left, and you can delve into what your competitors are up to. Fly to the right and you can zoom in on what you found when you benchmarked top-performing companies.

All this, and more, is available to help associates work smarter. Companies that want to take advantage of this type of tool need three things: (1) The technology (and the way things are heading, that's the easy part); (2) **The commitment to be user centered;** and (3) Techno-wonks with the freedom to design spaces that excite people.

"It's important to organize businesses around their knowledge structure, instead of their departmental structure."

ALDEN GLOBE
Intellectual Services Consultant
Knowledge Resource Strategies Group,
JD Edwards

"When you navigate through a company's information space, you're really navigating the commitments people make to each other."

HUBERT SAINT-ONGE
SVP, Strategic Capabilities
Clarica

continued from page 177

into performance systems (usually, what the company controls) and collaborative systems (what associates control). Then communicate that position to all associates, vendors, partners, and to the people designing these systems.

BUILDING THE CONNECTIONS BEHIND THE SCENES

Easy navigation doesn't happen just because you create an index for information or provide people with tools to search databases. A lot of hard work goes on behind the scenes to connect ideas and specific content.

Andersen Consulting is respected for its efforts in this area. Their Knowledge Xchange system and other approaches to knowledge management have won high praise because of how easily and quickly teammates can get in, get what they need, and get out. One of Andersen's consultants, Greg Pryor of the Global Work Processes team, explains why.

"We have folks called knowledge integrators," says Pryor. "They look for patterns and connections between different projects, and they help build those connections back into the system. It's a cultural discipline. The integrators are considered to be thought leaders in what they do. And they have a very different mix of work. They spend about 60 percent of their time doing integration/thought leadership work and about 40 percent doing client facing." [That's consultant-speak for working with clients.]

"I think the best consulting firms have three things that make for easier navigation," concludes Pryor. "First is an infrastructure designed for easy and simple sharing of knowledge. Second, there are key players whose role is to make connections between everything—like our integrators. Third is competency. It takes a unique set of skills to be inquisitive and see patterns where most people see only noise, and then to be able to integrate that information rapidly into what you're doing."

DESIGN NOTES: Pryor's comments reflect one of the most critical behind-the-scenes activities in all great navigation systems. Somebody spends a lot of time thinking about content—what connects this idea to that, what are the things that most of us miss, etc.

Yet, outside of consultancies like Andersen and some high-tech firms, few companies are investing in infomediaries—teams of people who add value by helping to sort, prioritize, and find *user-centered* patterns and connections. As we saw in Chapter 11, many navigational problems happen because there are so few resources dedicated to making sense of things *before* they go into corporate e-spaces. Making it easy to surf through noise and clutter isn't really what navigation is about.

GETTING STARTED: Look at Pryor's three-point plan: (1) Don't worry about the technology. Competitive pressures and e-commerce will force you to build what's necessary. (2 & 3) Focus on the things that happen behind the technology. Do you have teams of people—integrators, infomediaries, whatever-you-want-to-call-them—to build user-centered content? And, as at Andersen, are they highly valued thought leaders? Are you developing and paying for the skills you need to build the content all associates need to work smarter?

THREE STORIES ABOUT THINKING BIGGER THAN E-SPACES: A LOT BIGGER

How Your Associates Define Integration

Larry Keeley is obsessed with simplicity: "A great strategy can usually be diagrammed on the back of a business card and has a single major point: What you are going to do to constructively alter the daily lives of millions of people?" He also believes in the power of working backwards from people's needs: "Unfortunately, those who craft strategy usually aren't curious enough about people's everyday lives. This is always the best starting place for true breakthroughs."

Keeley is president of the Doblin Group, a Chicago-based strategic design planning firm. The Doblin Group merges the disciplines of strategic planning and design to develop product and business innovations.

"Take a look at these areas," says Keeley. "Massive budgets are

spent on the following things:
- Knowledge management
- Group and individual information worktools
- Corporate training and learning
- Facilities
- Audio-visual systems
- Telecommunications

"You'll find all of them are interesting frontiers associated with rapid innovation. But, most of the people who manage the budgets for these things are in separate domains and often do not talk to each other. It's not uncommon to find that a CIO has a huge budget for knowledge management that is completely unrelated to a parallel budget for facilities and designing the right kind of work spaces."

Keeley continued, "We're currently trying to stitch together a group of noncompetitive companies to research what is possible when all these things are viewed as one integrated whole. If we do this right, we believe we'll find new ways to create entirely new environments that are a blast to go to—where human beings will collaborate much more effectively. The walls and the information systems will keep track of what's going on, and the total information space will help people make simpler, smarter decisions. The trick is working backwards from what people need to attend to, then bringing together the best practices from very separate technologies and approaches."

DESIGN NOTES: Keeley is talking about taking a fresh look at your company the way associates experience it. For most people, their company is a big information space where lots of things should work together, but don't. And when he mentions people not talking to each other, he's going beyond insiders to include all the outside vendors that could be developing common platforms and solutions, but aren't. He believes that often "the true innovators at the edges of these frontiers don't even know each other."

GETTING STARTED: Take two or three people from each department/ discipline listed by Keeley and lock them in a room for several days. Interrupt them only once with a parade of associates explaining how they try to collaborate with each other. See what the team comes up with. If their efforts don't create substantial cost savings and new ways for associates to navigate through all the noise, lock them up again. This time for a month.

Smart Rooms: A Glimpse at the Future of Navigation

Meet Marshall Woolard and Dave Martin. They work for different companies more than a thousand miles apart. Martin is CEO of Smart Technologies in Calgary, Canada. His technology is on the walls at Texas Instruments, where Woolard works for TI's Collaboration and Knowledge Sharing team. Together, they are building smart rooms.

"We build interactive white boards," says Martin. "Our technology lets an entire wall become an interactive touchscreen. Not only can you write on it and have the writing captured digitally, but you can retrieve and use files from a company database, intranet, or website and project them on the wall, using it like a huge monitor. This type of technology is more and more important as less work is done at people's desks. Intel has tracked that they have about 11 million minutes of meetings each month and 70 percent of people's time is not spent at their desks."

In a separate conversation, Woolard picked up on that point. "When we were looking at how to build our smart rooms, Intel said it best. They compared conference room experiences to going into the middle of the Mojave Desert to have a meeting. You don't have your files, often you can't plug into the network—a lot of what you needed is back in your office. Yet people spend a large portion of their time in conference rooms expecting to do real work."

Woolard continued, "In 1998 we started creating what we call smart rooms. The goal is for the technology to be as transparent as possible. You can't get much more transparent than writing on a wall! People can present ideas or brainstorm however they feel comfortable, and everything is saved and retrievable in Web formats."

"We're finding that initial project meetings take 50 to 75 percent longer because you have a lot more at your fingertips. But the extra time means that everything gets integrated from the start. Previously, we might have had three different meetings with subteams going off and tackling assignments. Instead all that work comes together in the first meeting. This way of working is especially beneficial when people are conferenced in from smart rooms in different cities," concludes Woolard.

DESIGN NOTES: For lots of people reading this book, smart rooms are just too high-tech and cost too much to think about right now. (It's fantasy: "I know that on 'Star Trek' they can walk up to the walls anywhere in the ship and interact with anyone or anything. But that's science fiction.") There are two important takeaways from TI's smart rooms that are not fiction: (1) We are about to cross the point where *everything*, including walls, is intelligent—with chips and computing power built right into their surfaces; (2) All that power means diddly squat unless we're prepared to use it.

Simpler companies will be prepared. They are already thinking about building a common visual language for telling people how to get more information; or creating common ways to link and compare projects, workloads, and strategies. Within the next few years simpler companies will spend as much time thinking about navigational comparisons, pathways, maps, hierarchies—even color schemes— as they now spend on how to communicate the strategic plan.

Most companies aren't thinking about these things because the little box that sits on everyone's desks has some form of navigation built into it. Layers of information, relationships between ideas, and the links between content are restricted by the software and networks we use.

Well, navigation is about to bust out of that little box. Smart paper clips are now in the works. Many lecture halls have smart armrests. Name badges can currently track you anywhere in the building. The total physical environment is becoming an information space.

For some people, busting out of the box will make it a lot easier to work smarter. It will be wildly liberating. For many, if someone isn't thinking about navigation, it could feel like trying to find a firefly in Las Vegas at night.

GETTING STARTED: Let's not go overboard. For most of us, completely smart physical spaces are years away. But you should still round up the people Larry Keeley talked about in the previous story. Do lock them in a room. And ask them one question: "If a lot more of the environment is going to be an information space within two to five years, what navigation tools, languages, and structures should we be thinking about now?" Focus them specifically on the changes that will help knowledge workers get in, get what they need, and get out.

Smart Walls: The Very Low-Tech Kind

Here's a pair who haven't worked together but share a common view. Christine Albertini is head of research and development at Steelcase Furniture. Clement Mok is chief creative officer at Sapient. They believe in a very low-tech version of smart walls.

FRAMEWORK FOR THINKING ABOUT NAVIGATION

Most of us don't think about navigation because it's built into that little box on our desks. We need to. Because most of us travel way outside that box—into an environment with no common maps, pointers, or pathways—for the things we need to work smarter.

CONTENT DISCIPLINE	NAVIGATION CRITERIA	WHAT WILL CHANGE TO BE USER CENTERED
Information Architecture	**Clear, Consistent Access:** The organization of ideas is consistent, persistent, and easy to find	• **PREDICTABILITY:** Getting any information should be intuitive; the structure was designed backwards from people's needs • **PROGRESSION:** Everything is consistently layered from simplest level to most detailed. No user should get more than he or she wants
Information Design	**Clear Directions:** Prompts, guides, tutorials, and instructions are consistent, hard to miss, and easy to use	• **VISIBILITY:** In any environment, directions, tutorials, and system controls should mean the same things all the time • **TRANSPARENCY:** Content and structures must reflect what you are trying to achieve. Imposed structures (like the strategic plan) need to be linked but should stay in the background.
Worktool Design	**Clear, Useful Content:** Structured for personal success and effective, respectful use of your time	• **APPROPRIATENESS:** You should get exactly what you need for your task • **GIVE, GET, MANIPULATE:** It should be just as easy for you to manipulate content as it is for you to input and retrieve information • **FEEDBACK:** Any action should have an immediate and obvious effect

Several of the categories and definitions on this page are based upon ideas from Clement Mok's *Designing Business* (Adobe Press, 1996).

Albertini: "A lot of the complexity in the work world comes from not being able make to make critical connections between ideas or information. Because of that, my team has studied what enables exemplary decision making. One of the key things we've found is what we call 'information persistence'—teams need dedicated workrooms where the walls reflect their thinking. If people can leave their work up and continually come back to it, the room itself facilitates rapid decision making."

Mok: "One of the biggest factors we've found in team success is getting project schedules up on the wall, not unlike a train schedule. Is everything on time? The very fact that there's a big piece of paper on the wall, that is changed with markers and stickey notes, helps people understand the dynamics of what's going on in real time. It's not the same if you go to the Internet, pull down a report, and print it out. That's too abstract. Having the project schedule up on the wall, with names attached to deadlines, is very powerful, very clear."

DESIGN NOTES: All design firms and production shops know this. Apparently, corporate architects do not. Because in much of Corporate America, very little wall space can be found to create Albertini's information persistence or Mok's project schedule. This seems silly because it is a big-win, low-cost way of making it simpler for people to succeed. Surrounding people with clear, easy-to-use specifics is also a basic tenet of any quality initiative.

GETTING STARTED: Rebel. Tape paper over everything. Post ideas, schedules, and roles anywhere, using every bit of wall space you're not supposed to. Here's a hint for the really big schedules: Go to a commercial printer that does 36-inch or wider web printing. They use paper that is spooled onto huge rolls, and when they switch rolls, there's always 50 to 100 yards left over. If you smile nicely when you ask for one, they might even give it to you for free.

Making It Simpler to Succeed

Navigation, especially in today's overloaded environment, is a basic human need for success.

Simpler companies will go beyond the basics. They will understand that there are compelling competitive reasons to make it easy for people to get into systems, get what they need, and get out. If it's true that people are the only real competitive advantage, then navigation is all about maximizing your most important asset.

There is no limit to the different tools, techniques, and ways of creating easy navigation. So don't look for a cookbook list of instructions. Instead, try to understand the guiding principles and ideas behind what makes for helpful, useful navigation.

Most companies need to broaden their view of navigation. We need to start looking at our organizations the way our associates experience them—as big information spaces with no common maps, guideposts, or languages. The goal isn't to overmanage or try to solve for all the needs. Instead, when thinking about navigation, walk through your company with your associates' eyes and look at what needs to change to make it easier for people to work smarter.

Most important, easy and awesome navigation is about trust. Whenever you hand someone a well-designed map, you are letting them guide themselves through the terrain. Anything in your company that is hard to navigate—even unintentionally—sends the message "Don't trust us to help you work smarter."

Simpler companies will make it easier for more people to navigate more of the company. And those people will trust them more.

PROTOTYPING THE FUTURE OF NAVIGATION

Do you have a concierge desk at your company? How about a dry cleaner or convenience store? To enhance productivity, lots of companies are arranging for services like these. (If you don't have to run that errand in the middle of the day, that's another half-hour available for work.) One global consulting firm even has a service that waters teammates' plants and drops their cars off for repairs.

Corporate America seems to be caring a lot more about you and your time. **Then why aren't** we seeing more services dedicated to one of the largest drains on your time—navigating the noise so you can find the stuff you need to work smarter?

Why aren't Knowledge Concierge Desks or Knowledge Call Centers popping up everywhere? Human nature keeps proving that when people need help with complicated problems (like knowledge work), most of us want **to talk to another person**—with as little computer interface as possible.

One model might be the GE Answer Center. Consumers call the center when they need help with a specific problem. Tele-helpers search databases for solutions and direct the customer to additional people who can help. The tele-helpers stay on the line until they get you the help you need, and they are available anytime, any day. Another model might be www.answers.com. Its database is like many you will find on the Web, but the search engine is real people who chat with you, trade emails with you, and send you answers and sources for additional help.

The reason we are not seeing services like these everywhere is another case of corporate logic triumphing over human nature. From the company's perspective, it's more cost-effective to let people use databases and search engines.

The key question is not which should triumph— human nature or corporate logic. It is: Will companies hit a threshold where it becomes critical for everyone in a diverse population to work a lot smarter—not just the people who are good with databases?

"Easy navigation is about leadership. Because how people answer their own questions is a test of an organization's commitment to deal with all the unnecessary complexity and noise."

MARK KOSKINIEMI
VP, Human Resources
Buckman Labs

"This is not about understanding every choice we face. That's impossible.
This is about the fact that there will be [individual] winners and losers. The number of people we are losing due to complex choices may not be acceptable. Both in employment turnover and in society at large."

GREG NADEAU, Chief Information Officer
Massachusetts Department of Education

Simpler FutureWork

Rethinking how we spend our tomorrows. What if we took the two main ideas behind simplicity further? What if we changed how companies are structured in order to 1) use time differently, and 2) work backwards from what people need?

Simple companies would **change one of today's most basic assumptions.**

Work, even in the flattest, most empowering, most innovative companies, is based on **answers.**

Someone or some team is charged with letting the
rest of us know: This is how we should be structured
to meet marketplace and customer needs....
This is what each business unit should focus on....
This is how to we should staff those units....
This is how we'll integrate everything. They have to
be nimble, focused, and godlike enough to keep their
solutions fresh on a monthly, weekly—even daily—
basis. This approach either sets up leaders for failure
or our associates for tons of unnecessary complexity.

In Chapter 14, you will meet SimpliCorp, a fictitious
company launched sometime in the future. The
company figured out that its biggest time waster was
trying to get everyone connected to the answers that
some leadership team had come up with. So the
company's structure is based on **questions.**

At SimpliCorp, budgets are assigned to projects, not business units. And no project gets started until associates have used toolkits to answer questions like: What business are we in? What does our customer need today? How do we create value?
The answers they create for themselves help them **navigate** a world filled with infinite choices.

It would be foolish to propose SimpliCorp as the model of the future. This fictional setting makes no predictions. Instead, this book ends as it began. The goal of Chapter 14 is to suggest new ways to discuss what it means to lead and work smarter. From those conversations, a simpler future will emerge.

FUTUREWORK PRE-WORK

Structure is not organization.
> **Robert Waterman,** author

When you have eliminated the impossible, whatever remains, however improbable, must be the truth.
> **Sherlock Holmes,** sleuth

It is possible to identify and prepare for the future that has already happened.
> **Peter Drucker,** sage

We are confronted with insurmountable opportunities.
> **Pogo,** possum

CHAPTER 14

Lead Through Navigation

Changing how we structure companies

DATELINE:	Several tomorrows from now
PLACE:	Orientation camp for SimpliCorp, a leader in knowledge products for niche markets and emerging industries
PLAYERS:	Tamara: Orientation Guide and Coach
	Eduardo: Division President-in-training
	Diane: Content Specialist-in-training
SCENE:	There are 127 people at this orientation session. Tamara is one of the guides whose role is to be available for one-on-one and small-group discussions, to help people answer their own questions.

We are about to eavesdrop on some conversations at SimpliCorp's weeklong orientation camp. Each of the "simplinauts," as the trainees jokingly refer to themselves, arrived with different expectations.

Eduardo was hired away from SimpliCorp's biggest competitor to refocus and lead one of the company's business units. His views might be called "old school." When recruited to join SimpliCorp, he was comfortable with the company's culture, even while he believed he knew best how to organize his division. After all, fast and continuous restructuring is one of his strengths—knowing just when and how to shift gears. He figures that he'll learn enough about SimpliCorp during orientation to impose his way of working on his business unit.

Instead, the week's activities will impose upon him. More than 50 percent of the leaders-in-training wash out during orientation. They are not prepared for the shift in control. SimpliCorp believes that markets and consumer needs are shifting so rapidly that no leadership team can figure out how to restructure fast enough. So the company moved the process for making those shifts into the hands of the people who are

SimpliCorp's Restructuring Process

1 **All work begins** by answering core questions like: What business are we in? How do we create value? What do our customers want?

1. CORE QUESTIONS

TOOLKITS

2 To answer the questions, SimpliCorp has built **toolkits** to help people **navigate** daily changes. Toolkits include knowledge clusters as well as how-to checklists, maps, people directories, best practices, etc.

2. NAVIGATION

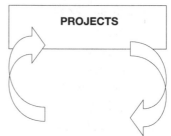

PROJECTS

3 Mostly, the toolkits help associates simplify everyday work. But they also help them **restructure themselves** by submitting designs to the Executive Council.

3. BUDGETING / RESOURCING

PROJECT PORTFOLIOS
Managed by an Executive Council

4 The foundation for all of this is the Council's commitment to unbundle or rebundle the components parts of the company as needed. They are no longer locked into the business unit model, because they are no longer locked into one way of building these components.

4. CREATE A NEW COMPANY EVERY DAY

THREE COMPANY COMPONENTS*
Customer Relationship Management
Product Innovation
Infrastructure Management

*From: John Hagel III and Marc Singer of McKinsey & Company

doing the work. Front-line associates—in fact, anyone in the organization—can propose changes, in the form of projects to be funded by leadership teams. This is just too big a leap for some leaders.

Diane is the ultimate get-it-done person. Her mantra is, "Give me a deadline, a goal, and turn me loose."

She's joining SimpliCorp as a content specialist. Her role will be to develop and maintain the toolkits people use to get work done. She's about to learn new kinds of questions to ask before leaping into action—because the toolkits she'll be building must consistently help everyone at SimpliCorp work smarter and faster.

Changing the Rules of the Game

The aha's experienced by the simplinauts can be a springboard for present-day discussions. For all our talk about nimbleness, speed, smashing boundaries, and changing the rules, one assumption still remains: It is *leadership's* role to structure. And restructure. And restructure. And restructure.

In all other aspects of decision making, leaders are saying, "The world has gotten too complex. Nobody has enough of the answers to make decisions from above. We need to push decision making to the front lines." Yet somehow we expect these same leaders to be smart enough to know how to structure business units that can meet consumer needs and can take on all competitors. Smart enough to know how to budget for and staff these business units. Smart enough to know how to integrate everything.

Nobody's that smart.

Mix in marketplace volatility, and leaders almost have to be godlike to succeed—comparing company structures to marketplace needs on a monthly, weekly, even daily basis, and taking the right action.

Nobody's that good.

If we keep assuming that leaders can stay one step ahead of the need to restructure, we are either setting them up for failure or setting up everyone in their organizations for tons of unnecessary work complexity.

SimpliCorp takes a stab at spreading the smartness around.

As you read, take note of the diagram on page 196, "SimpliCorp's Restructuring Process." The discussions between Eduardo, Diane, and Tamara provide clues about how it is put into practice.

Using Time Differently

"Tamara, can you help me with a few things?" Eduardo asked.
"Shoot," she replied.

"I just left the session that described how SimpliCorp funds only projects, not business units. I have to admit that I came here thinking I could work around this idea. But when five other division presidents reviewed the details of how budgets are used to develop project portfolios, I heard a wake-up call! A lot of what I know about restructuring isn't going to help me. Can we talk about how this works?"

"Sure, but first let's back up," said Tamara. "In your session, did they talk about the average time between restructurings for companies like ours?"

"Yeah. It's now about eight months, projected to hit six by year's end. That's exactly why I'm here! Whadda rush—reinventing ourselves every six months."

"That's why I'm here, too," replied Tamara. "But what does all that restructuring do to your ability to execute the strategy? If we stick with typical budgeting and business unit structures, every 180 days people will find out that they're in Division Y instead of Division X. Or that there's a new strategic plan to be followed. By the time everybody hears what the new strategy is, they've been restructured again. Or six months after you arrive there might even be a new division president with new ideas about how to get things done."

"OK, I get the point. But if I don't have control of budgeting and how and when to restructure, I—"

"You do have control over budgets," Tamara jumped in. "But not restructuring. We pushed that a lot closer to the marketplace. In your session they talked about the Executive Council, right? Well, you and 18 members of the Council—in most other companies, you'd be called division presidents—still have budgetary and profit and loss accountabilities. But instead of old-style business unit budgets and plans, you act like VCs—venture capitalists. Associates go through a disciplined process for developing projects, and they come to you for funding, just like entrepreneurs seeking seed money. Your job is to pick the right projects that will help you make Plan. This includes projects that call for outsourcing just about anything. With very few exceptions, you're not locked into a specific infrastructure."

"So, I've got to start thinking like a VC…"

"You got it," encouraged Tamara.

" …Which means you don't need my restructuring skills," Eduardo said, "because most of the structure is coming from the people closest to the action. That still makes me uncomfortable." Eduardo wasn't fully sold, but he was seeing new possibilities.

"There is an advantage, though," he continued. "You talked about people having to learn a new strategy or be taught what a new leader wants every six months. But SimpliCorp's approach eliminates all that. We can move a lot faster because the ideas and structures are coming from everywhere instead of just from the Executive Council. Nobody's waiting for me to announce how the next restructuring affects them."

Once he got the basics of the idea, Eduardo wanted to dig deeper. "If I'm gonna lead a business unit using this process, I've got to be damned sure our associates can generate the right kind of projects. Tell me how that works."

"I've got a better idea," said Tamara. "The session that would answer your question just started. You might want to get over there."

DESIGN NOTES: The model for the Executive Council is not new. Besides VCs, many firms create entrepreneurial environments where execs can invest seed monies in new ventures. (For a terrific overview of present-day companies that use the model—Shell, Virgin, GE Capital, Monsanto and others—see "Bringing Silicon Valley Inside," by Gary Hamel in the September/October 1999 issue of *Harvard Business Review*.)

SimpliCorp has added a twist to present-day approaches. It has turned the whole idea of what it means to structure a company upside down. Instead of everyone looking to the Executive Council for the next big change, SimpliCorp has replaced business units with a structure that puts the responsibility for change with the people on the front lines, providing them with toolkits and processes to make it work.

There are three basic components to any company—customer relationship management, product innovation, and infrastructure management. The secret to success is to avoid getting so dependent on any one component that you can't quickly spin it off or rebuild it. The diagram on page 196 describes SimpliCorp's approach as a commitment to being flexible enough to bundle and unbundle these components as needed.

John Hagel III and Marc Singer, principals of McKinsey & Company, detailed the components of any company and bundling/unbundling in their book, *Net Worth: Shaping Markets When Customers Make the Rules*. But their approach focused mainly on executives. SimpliCorp added an important dimension to their model, by looking at how all associates can help drive the process.

If you do not directly involve associates in the process of restructuring your company, you'll look back on today's sources of complexity with fondness. As change happens faster and becomes more volatile, many associates—far more than we want to admit—will end up spending most of their time trying to figure out what the structure-of-the-day means to them. Execution could become as unpredictable as market forces.

> *Platitudes aside, our biggest limit is no longer the reach of our imagination. It's our ability to order, make sense of, and connect everything demanding our attention. Our biggest limit is our ability to create clarity as quickly as we change.*

Customers and competitors may write the rules of the marketplace, but the Attention Economy drives execution. You will only be able to go as fast as it takes people to figure out what the latest change means. Restructure all you want, just know that execution travels at the speed of sense-making.

Tomorrow's simpler companies will change how time gets used because they will eliminate a huge, unnecessary step. When associates no longer have to wait for leaders to restructure the company—when they drive the process—everything makes sense a whole lot faster.

Working Backwards

On day three of orientation week, Diane went looking for Tamara. Diane needed help in making connections between some of the ideas she was hearing about.

"Tamara, overall I'm really jazzed," Diane began. "The people are great. Everything I'm learning says I want to spend a long time with this company. But some things aren't clicking for me. Like this whole Core Questions thing. It seems so warm and fuzzy."

She showed Tamara a single piece of paper. On it was written:

Core Company Questions

• What business are we in?
• How do we create value?
• How do we define success?
• What do we value?

Core Division Questions

• What does our customer need today?
• How do we define success?

Core Personal Questions

• How do I define success?
• How will I create value?
• How will I get it done?

Tamara responded with a question: "Diane, what's our company mission?"

Diane recited the words—everyone could recite them by the end of day one—but clearly, she didn't fully grasp their meaning.

"One of the things we've learned over the years," Tamara responded, "is that with so much change happening so fast, it's easy to lose the spirit of the mission. So we tried to mimic human nature. In most new situations, the first thing anybody does is ask questions like the ones you've written down. Everything at SimpliCorp works backwards from those questions."

"The questions direct you to the toolkits we've built. The toolkits help you come up with your own answers, but they also—"

Diane finished Tamara's sentence: "They generate conversations about SimpliCorp's mission, vision, values, and business objectives. That means we can create our own clarity during any restructuring. We don't have to wait for the Executive Committee to come down from the mountain with the official tablets."

"Exactly," said Tamara. She quickly followed up with another question. "As a Content Specialist, you'll develop a lot of what goes into those toolkits. Over the past couple days, have you thought about what it's gonna take to build toolkits that work?"

"Yeah! I was blown away by how many alliance partners and freelance contractors are part of the company. I never would have guessed that almost two-thirds don't work here full-time. That means my content and the tools have to be intuitive and easy to use. I can't assume that everybody is up on the latest SimpliCorp changes or that one tool will be used by everybody in the same way."

Diane continued, "Navigation is also huge. Anybody, anywhere needs to be able to find whatever they need quickly."

From there, Diane's get-it-done personality took over. She started scribbling some of her ideas on the whiteboard walls. A crowd gathered and joined in. Tamara smiled to herself when Diane briefly stopped the brainstorming to ask, "Wait. Is this changing what business we're in?"

DESIGN NOTES: SimpliCorp has chosen two ways to apply "working backwards" to their organizational structure.

1. All work starts with human nature, not corporate logic.
Since people instinctively ask questions when they want to make sense of a new situation, SimpliCorp formalized that process. They built upon the work of strategists Gary Hamel and C. K. Prahalad, who introduced the idea that companies need to develop and focus on their "core competencies"—the skills and capabilities that are most important to a company's success.

When SimpliCorp married the idea of core competencies to working backwards, it came up with "core questions." It believes that the answers to these questions determine how people work and create. As the simplinauts gain experience, the core questions become more useful to them and can be adapted to more varied situations. For example: "What business are we in?" can be a no-brainer if the work being done is a continuation of previous strategies. But, during major changes in structure and corporate strategy, this question brings out subtleties that are often buried—resulting in more understanding, sense-making and radically altering the speed of execution.

2. After years of being user centered, SimpliCorp began to see patterns and clusters in what associates needed to work smarter. It built toolkits to address these needs. These toolkits include knowledge clusters—groupings of content that are often compared or used together—pre-packaged guides, references, checklists, sources, etc. All are based on the specific tasks people are trying to accomplish. Although no one is forced to use the toolkits—in fact, some of the best innovations came when associates ignored them—for most daily work, they have greatly simplified execution.

All the toolkits are mapped to the core questions. Since those questions create less than a dozen ways to begin any process, SimpliCorp associates can easily find and use the pathways, guides, and connections among the toolkits. Navigation becomes a lot easier.

In fact, toolkit creation became such a strong competency, it was spun off as a business unit. In the same way that today's companies might send people to the Disney Institute, many of tomorrow's firms attend the SimpliCorp Toolkit Center.

All this, and more, was possible because SimpliCorp is dedicated to one idea:

> *People have limitless capacity to work smarter.*
> *As long as what you build is user centered.*

Tomorrow's simpler companies will go beyond adapting systems to help people work smarter. They will take on one of the last bastions of control—how the company gets structured—and move it a lot closer to the people who do the work.

To accomplish this—without blowing up the company—we need to change a basic assumption. Why aren't we letting the people who do the work figure out the best way to structure themselves and their work? The only reason we assume that it is leadership's role to restructure the company is that we've never let anyone else participate. Therefore, we've never built anything—infrastructures, tools, processes, etc.—so that associates could contribute.

When we begin, in earnest, to be user centered and work backwards from the needs of our workforce, there will be no limits to what is possible.

The Power to Do More and Less

The story of SimpliCorp is no prediction. Who knows, it could be flat-out wrong. No one knows how we will spend our tomorrows. But some guiding principles have already emerged. One of them is: Whoever is faster at changing the rules will win more often.

This book is about changing the rules so people have the power to do less of what doesn't matter and more of what does. This means we have to start changing two habits that create work complexity and confusion:

- We need to **use time differently** by changing how we organize and share what we know—how we create meaning and make sense of things.
- We need to **work backwards from what people need** to work smarter. Most everyone is a lot smarter than we are letting them be.

These ideas will make some people uncomfortable. When you first mention "simplicity" to them, they all scream, "We need some of that!" Then reality hits. Simplicity is about creating clarity through ideas, not corporate edict. Simplicity challenges our assumptions about control— much more needs to be closer to the front lines.

All of which makes simplicity as much about leadership as anything else.

Lucy Fellowes provides some powerful leadership lessons for a world filled with infinite choices. In the early 1990s, she was curator of an exhibit at the Cooper-Hewitt Museum titled *The Power of Maps*. This is what she wrote about the exhibit:

> In making maps, we find ways through spaces physical or metaphorical; through problems; through realms of information. Maps testify to our extraordinary ability to visualize as we seek order and meaning….Maps allow us to see even the invisible: places remote, vast or deep; connections between people…and events;…causes and consequences.
>
> Maps give us overview and insight. For those who have access to them, maps can be agents of change. Bringing change about is as much a matter of consciousness as it is of tools and technology.
>
> By understanding the persuasive power of maps, we can go on to use them to make sense of the world and our place in it locally, regionally and globally. Somewhere, the map you need exists, or can be made now.

We will create simpler companies when our leaders—including you, me and anyone else who is trying to get things done through people—see themselves as mapmakers of the world as it is, not just as their strategic plan sees it. The change will start to happen when they begin making invisible connections between people, actions, and events visible. And when they build infrastructures that are as much about sense-making as they are about getting things done.

When we create those simpler companies, we will be leading through navigation. We will be making it simpler for everyone to succeed because we'll be building companies where people can guide themselves through a world of infinite choices.

The Power to Do What's Important

As I worked on this book...

My son's teeth were straightened with braces more advanced and less painful than anything you or I endured. My beautiful niece was born six weeks premature. A woman I hardly know emailed to renege on being interviewed for the book. She just discovered she had breast cancer.

Compared to our health and well-being, simplicity isn't worth mentioning.

Many friends spent too many hours away from their families.

Compared to family, simplicity is not important.

World Bank president Jim Wolfensohn spoke at the Conference Board's annual dinner. He said: "There is...a human drama that rarely gets headlines....We have 3 billion people in the world who live on under $2 a day. We have 1.3 billion people that live on under $1 a day. We have 1.5 billion people who don't have access to clean water. We have another 2 billion who don't have power. We're losing forests at the rate of an acre a second....In another 30 years, we're going to need twice the food, with no greater arable land."

Compared to the well-being of our neighbors and the planet, the topic of this book is irrelevant.

Simplicity becomes important only when we stop to consider all the truly amazing discoveries and advances that did not happen today. Or how many opportunities for personal, corporate, and community growth didn't fit into today's 1,440 minutes. All because of the convoluted ways we used people's time and attention.

Endnotes

For lots more resources, notes, sources, research data (including a downloadable copy of the 146-page "Search for a Simpler Way" study), and chatspaces dedicated to simplicity, please visit this book's c companion: **http://www.simplerwork.com.**

Chapter 1
1. "The Age of Social Transformation," *The Atlantic Monthly,* November 1994, pp. 53-80.
2. "The Next Information Revolution," *Forbes ASAP,* April 24, 1998, pp. 47-58.

Chapter 2
1. "Education and the Economy: An Indicators Report," U.S. Bureau of Labor Statistics, p. xviii, www.nab.com/econ/index.html
2. "Thrashed by the Real World," *Forbes ASAP,* April 7, 1997, www.forbes.com/asap
3. "24-7," *Forbes ASAP,* November 30, 1998, www.forbes.com/asap

Chapter 3
1. July 1999 Bureau of Labor Statistic (BLS) data.

Chapter 8
1. Joseph Campbell, *The Power of Myth,* (New York: Doubleday, 1988), p. 4.
2. "Driving Change: An Interview with Ford Motor Company's Jacques Nasser," *Harvard Business Review* (March/April 1999): 82-83.

Chapter 11
1. John Brockman, *Digerati: Encounters with the Cyber Elite,* (San Francisco: HardWired, 1996), p. 87.
2. In Chapter 1, Gavin Kerr was quoted as saying, "People tolerate management's logic, but they act on their own conclusions." Kerr's inspiration was one of the very first uses of Root Learning's Learning Maps.

Thank You

All right everyone, line up alphabetically according to your height.

Casey Stengel, Yogi Berra's only peer in eloquence

Time for the real authors of Simplicity to step up. For the most part, I was along for the ride. These are the people who made this book possible.

Family. This book centers on caring about how we use people's time and attention. Louise, my wife, and Ian, my son, generously shared the most precious thing they have - our time together. Their love, selflessness, teasing, laughter, and patience gave me the time to make sense occasionally. Thanks Beez. Thank you Ian.

Work-in-Progress Readers. Once the pages were no longer blank, these people took my babbling ramblings and suggested ways to compose clearer thoughts. Don Barry, Larry Belle, Rick Bradley, Tony Cortese, Allan Csiky, Donna Davenport, Dave DeSantis, Dan Distelhorst, Susan Fehl, Barbara Gannett, Chris Grygo, Michael Havens, Pat Kenealy, Mike Kinney, Mark Koskiniemi, Rick Ritacco, John Santoro, Jim Shanley and Sue Wright - I owe you more than I can ever say. Thanks!

Book Teammates. About 500 times a day Nick Philipson, my editor, cheerfully answered his phone and my questions, insisting I was his favorite author. (I'm sure at least once or twice he really meant it.) Thank you Nick, so much. Behind the scenes at Perseus, three people's unwavering support brought this book from idea to reality. Elizabeth Carduff, Chris Coffin, and David Goehring: Thank you!

"Agent" is so inadequate. Yes, Lisa Adams and David Miller found our study on the Net and said "You should write a book about this."

And yes, they connected me with Perseus. But they also toiled as counselors, sounding boards, editors, coaches, guides and shrinks. Lisa and David, you're the best!

Design and Production. Aimee Leary at Iowa Street Design made my paper napkin doodles come to life as the pages of this book. And Matt Versaggi did the same for the e-companion site, www.simplerwork.com. Thank you both for making it all happen, and making the complex clear.

Book Interviewees. Beginning in late 1998, over 125 people generously answered my emails and phone calls, and let me badger them in person. The people you met throughout this book, and who are listed in the index, deserve your highest praise. Their stories, ideas, and voices are what simplicity is all about.

Study Participants and Teammates. The ride began more than seven years ago with over 2500 "The Search for a Simpler Way" participants from more than 460 companies. Their ideas, needs, and concerns pointed the way. Please visit our website for a complete listing of participating companies, 25 tireless students and instructors at Northern Illinois University College of Business, and all the Jensen Group teammates who always delivered the impossible. Thanks guys!

Inspiration. Finally, this book would not have been possible if I hadn't stood on the shoulders of giants. Hundreds of thought leaders' and authors' ideas built the foundation for *Simplicity*. Too many to list here. However, three deserve special mention. Alvin Toffler helped me understand power in the Third Wave. Meg Wheatley helped me look at chaos and complexity in ways I never could have imagined. And Richard Saul Wurman helped me think about clarity, meaning and understanding from Jane and Joe Workforce's perspective.

Subject Index

Subject Index

S

Search for a Simpler Way
  Study, 10, 13, 19–33
Simplicity, 8–18
  basis of, 11
  clientele for, 16, 18
  in context, 207
  defined, 2
  discipline and, 16
  disciplines of, 124, 126
  distinguished from the
    simplistic, 12
  dollar value of, 38–39
  essence of, 17
  misconceptions about,
    15
  prototyping for, 138–139
  recognizing, 106
  science of, 126–127
  technology and, 41
  why it works, 14, 16
Simplicity Manifesto, 1–3
Smart rooms, 183–184
Smart walls, 184, 186
Store Like Me, 144
Stories and storytelling
  anatomy of, 96
  aspects of, 89
  as business tool, 90–97,
    102–103
  and clarity, 97–98
  digital future of, 98–99
  integrative value of,
    99–100
  tips for, 100. 101
  value of, 93
Succeed model, 173
Success
  aspects of, 17, 25–28
  management of, 60–61
  navigation and, 175,
    186–187

personal, 174
raw materials of, 69

T

Tasks, and choices, 160–163
Teamwork, 41
Technology, as problem and
  solution, 41
Time, 46–61
  as asset, 2
  building blocks for using,
    49–50, 52–61, 80
  hypothetical case study of
    managing, 198–200
  managing, 17, 43–45, 204
  managing others', 47–50
Time pressure, 25, 31, 33
Tools, 56–57
  brain's role in using, 70
  Know, Feel, Do, 63–65,
    66–67
  Learning Maps, 147–149
  Message Map, 90
  MIRRIAM, 150–152, 154
  storytelling, 90–97,
    102–103
  Use to Succeed, 63–64,
    68–69
  using, 63–64, 66, 68–69
Transparency, 177, 180
Triggers, 59
Trust, 128–139
  aspects of, 128
  building, 124, 137
  importance of, 132–136
  urgency of, 136, 138–139

U

USA Today, 141
Use model, 141
Use to Succeed tool, 63–64,
  65, 68–69
User-centered operation
  designing, 120–122
  facilitating, 110–111,
    122–123
  importance of, 109, 118
  penalties for not building,
    126–127

W

Work
  aspects of, 19–21
  complexity of, 21–28,
    30–33
  designing for easy
    navigation, 172–179
Workday, simplifying, 2
Workforce
  content design for, 141
  and employment
    contract, 129
  and environment, 173
  incentives for, 39–40
  skills needed for,
    132–133
  and user-centered
    structure, 109
Working backwards, 2, 17,
  106–107, 124, 200–204
  case studies of, 113–120
  hypothetical case study
    of, 200–203
  strategy for, 109–110,
    112

People Index

Organizations Index

M

Massachusetts Department
of Education, 189
McKinsey & Co., 28, 41,
196, 200
Merck, 10, 56–57, 113, 150,
152–153
Microsoft, 10
MIT Media Lab, 178
Monsanto, 46–47, 156–157,
199
Motorola, 118
MTV, 150

N

NASA, 108, 110, 124, 172
NationsBank, 1
New York Stock Exchange,
178
Northern Illinois University,
10, 133

O

ODR, 28, 90
Ontario Science Centre,
8–9, 172

P

Pecos River Learning
Center, 28
Penn State University, 27,
96, 118
Pepsi New England, 14
PepsiCo, 9, 98
Pitney Bowes Financial
Services, 15, 87

R

Root Learning, 147
Rutgers University, 133

S

SAIC, 52
Sam's Warehouse Club,
91, 92
Santa Fe Center for
Emergent Strategies, 102
Sapient, 12, 96, 119, 134,
184
Saturn, 12
Scientific Communications
Group (Merck), 113
Sears, 32, 143–145
ServiceMaster, 10
Sharon High School, 131
Shell, 199
Skandia, 153, 176–177
Smart Technologies, 183
Society for Human Resource
Management, 28
Sodexho Marriott Services,
135
Southwest Airlines, 10, 126
Steelcase Furniture, 118, 184
Studio Archetype, 119
Sun Microsystems, 108

T

TED conferences, 142
Texas Instruments, 183
3M, 11

U

United States Air Force, 110
United States Army, 10
United States Marines, 126
United States Navy, 110
University of Michigan, 97
University of Pennsylvania
Health Systems, 14
University of Pennsylvania,
Organizational
Development Masters
Program of, 93

V

Virgin, 199

W

Warner-Lambert, 47, 87
Watson Wyatt, 57
Weaver Aerospace, 15, 108
World Bank, 207

X

Xerox Corporation, 10, 108,
135
Xerox PARC, 12, 98, 135

Y

Yale University, 140

Z

ZoomTown.com, 15, 97

The Stories Continue. Please visit this book's e-companion, http://www.simplerwork.com. There, in addition to chatspaces dedicated to simplicity, you will find interviews with:

Aly Abulleil, Founder, Aliah Inc.

Christine Albertini, Research and Development, Steelcase Furniture

Chris Anderson, Director of Compensation, Sears

Howard Batley, Business Simplification and Corporate University, Conoco

Gordon Boronow, COO, American Skandia

Cathy Carmody, Organizational Electrician (change agent)

Pehong Chen, President, BroadVision

David Coleman, Managing Director, Collaborative Strategies

Michael Corriveau, President, Ignorance Insight

Joseph Cothrel, VP, Research, Participate.com

Guido de Grefte, Managing Director, KPMG Netherlands

Lisa Dennis, President, Knowledgence Associates

Duncan Dickson, Consultant, previously Director of Casting, Disney

Richard Durr, Senior Manager, Learning Strategies, Motorola

Ray Fattel, Vendor Relationships, Chase Manhattan

Rita Glaze, Knowledge Manager, Monsanto

Alden Globe, Knowledge Resource Strategies Group, J.D.Edwards

Michael Goldstein, Youth Technology Entrepreneurs, Massachusetts Dept. of Education

Vic Guinasso, CEO, DHL Worldwide Express

Bill Hamman, President, Education Division Sodexho Marriott

Susan Hanley, Knowledge Manager, AMS

Patricia Hill, Knowledge Manager, Xerox

Gary Hudson, Advanced Cost Management, AlliedSignal

Dave Johnson, Head of Manufacturing, General Mills

Hank Jonas, Compensation and Organizational Effectiveness, Corning

Elise Kaplan, Internal Change Consultant, UPenn Health Systems

Mark Koskiniemi, VP, Human Resources, Buckman Labs

Andrius Kulikauskas, Director, Minciu Sodas Laboratory

Tom Kunz, Networked Learning and Support Center, Shell

Tom Land, Senior Manager, Training and Development, Motorola

Ellen Langer, author, *Mindful Learning*

Dorothy Leonard, Harvard Business
School Professor, author, *Wellsprings
of Knowledge*

Dill Lutz, author, *Doubloopoak*

Yogesh Malhotra, Founder, Brint.com

Beth Mlakinin, Director, Body Engineering,
Saturn

Jackie Michel, Knowledge Manager,
Monsanto

Bill Miller, author, *Flash of Brilliance*

Greg Nadeau, CIO, Massachusetts
Department of Education

Mike O'Brien, President, ZoomTown.com

Jim Ritchie-Dunham, President,
Strategic Decision Simulation Group

Charlie Rogers, Executive Development,
PepsiCo

Hubert Saint-Onge, SVP, Strategic
Capabilities, Clarica

Ron Schultz, Santa Fe Center for
Emergent Strategies

Steve Schneider, Quality Assurance,
Monarch Marking Systems

Tom Short, Knowledge Management
Consultant, IBM

Bob Speed, Knowledge Management
Consultant, previously with Unilever

JG Spender, Dean, School of
Management, NY Institute of Technology

Susan Stucky, Associate Director,
Institute for Research on Learning

Catherine Tilley, Brand Consultant,
Leo Burnett, UK

Hildra Trotter, Knowledge Process Leader,
DowAgro Sciences

Rick Tucci, Founder, Leap Technology

Bob Veazie, International Change and
Safety, Hewlett-Packard

Arian Ward, President/CEO,
Work Frontiers International